In the Spirit of Business

A Guide to Resolving Fears and Creating Harmony in Your Worklife

ROBERT ROSKIND

CELESTIAL ARTS
BERKELEY, CALIFORNIA

Portions from A Course in Miracles © *copyright 1975, reprinted by permission of the Foundation for Inner Peace, Inc., Post Office Box 1104, Glen Ellen, California 95442.*

Text and cover design by Ken Scott
Composition by Ann Flanagan Typography

Additional copies of this book may be ordered directly from the publisher. Send $8.95 plus $2.00 for shipping and handling (plus 50 cents for each additional book). California residents include local sales tax.

Celestial Arts Publishing
P.O. Box 7123
Berkeley, CA 94707

FIRST PRINTING 1992

Library of Congress Cataloging-in-Publication Data

Roskind, Robert
    In the spirit of business: a guide to resolving fears and creating miracles in your
    worklife / by Robert Roskind.
        p.   cm.
    ISBN 0-89087-677-0
    1. Success in business.   2. Quality of work life.   3. Work and family.   4. Self-
    actualization (Psychology)   I. Title.
    HF5386.R654   1992
    650.1–dc20   92-25062
                                                                                CIP

1   2   3   4   5   6   7   8   9   10   /   96   95   94   93   92

Acknowledgments

My thanks to the following people for their help:

To my wife Julia, who for four years listened to me talk about writing this book and never lost faith that I would;

Lisa Conrad, my editor, for her consistent fine tuning;

Sal Glynn of Celestial Arts, for his insights and willingness to disagree until we got it right;

Ken Scott, for the perfect cover and book design;

David Hinds and George Young of Celestial Arts and Ten Speed Press, who believed we might be on to something;

Tom Shugru and George Benedict, who kept reminding me that I could write this book;

Bryan Smithwick, who was willing to discuss my ideas for hours and even occasionally agree;

John Funkhouser, who lovingly and laughingly practices many of the principles of this book;

my cousins Bobby, Rick, Stanley, and Herb, who have always encouraged and supported me in my endeavors;

Harley Levitt, who has always been there, reminding me of my potential;

and to my daughter Alicia, who always waited patiently for her daddy to stop writing and come play.

Dedication

To my two favorite teachers,

MY FAMILY — Julia, Julie, and Alicia

&

A COURSE IN MIRACLES

Contents

The Path Home

Everyone in the modern business world yearns for a more balanced and meaningful work life. *In the Spirit of Business* reminds us that this is possible. Its purpose is to explain principles that can offer each of us the opportunity to have:

A career or job that we truly love and that uses our best talents.

•

Enough money to meet our needs.

•

A well-designed schedule with enough time to do an excellent job and have time for our families, friends, and ourselves.

•

Harmony in our business relationships.

•

Opportunity to have the highest integrity in all our business dealings.

•

An ability to grow and benefit from any "failure" or setback.

•

The resources to successfully complete each undertaking and make decisions leading to the good of all involved.

These principles are based both on my own experiences and understanding as well as on the series of books entitled *A Course in Miracles*. *A Course in Miracles* is a detailed self-study guide that teaches how to resolve fears through forgiveness, the process known as the miracle. It is not necessary that you read these books; there are many paths and *A Course in Miracles* is just one of them. *A Course* reminds us we live in a safe and benevolent Universe, where peace, happiness, and miracles can and do naturally occur.

Each chapter of *In the Spirit of Business* covers a distinct area of business life (working with others, family, ethics, money, and failure) and examines the emotions, particularly the fears, that operate in these areas and affect our decision making. Loving and practical principles are explained that can resolve fears, principles that can transform your work life. It is not crucial that you use or even agree with all of these principles; your own experience will demonstrate their truth to you.

Distilled to its essence, our motivation for all our endeavors in life is happiness and peace. Real peace is an enlivened state of being, unclouded by fear or conflict; it is the most energetic and joyous state available to us. To reach it, we must clarify and refine our decision-making processes; where we had once chosen fear and conflict, we now *choose* peace and happiness. The best choices we make are those that create the least amount of pain and conflict and the greatest peace. Conflict in any area simply reflects errors of choice. This book is about examining and reevaluating our choices.

Once we begin to resolve our fears, we will create miracles. Miracles are not just supernatural events such as parting waters or levitation. Miracles are any and every act of love and forgiveness. These miracles, these everyday acts of love, are occurring all around us; we just haven't recognized them yet. As we are released from our fears, our true nature of trust and love will emerge once again. Our true nature will create miracles.

> *A man is lost in the woods and desperately seeks a way out. He travels down one dead-end path after another. Several days pass until, exhausted and discouraged, he spots another man walking through the forest. With renewed hope, he approaches the other man and says, "I have been going down trails that lead nowhere for days looking for a way out of this forest and had almost given up. I am so glad I found you. Will you please lead me out of here?" The other man, also looking weary and confused, responds, "I'm lost, too. But if we share the dead-end paths we have each been down, then we can both get home much easier and faster." (from* The Talmud*)*

This is our predicament, lost in the woods, somewhat weary and disillusioned, but still hopeful. Fortunately, our paths have just crossed and we have found each other through this book. *In the Spirit of Business* describes the dead-end trails I have been down and a few signposts I see up ahead. It is up to you to use these tools, or signposts, to lead you out of the forest to your own natural state or peace and happiness. Your own experience will establish the validity of these tools. All you need is an open mind to see for yourself the lights shining toward Home.

No one is in your life by accident, as a punishment, or as a trial to be endured. No one is in your life without a specific purpose and learning goal. Some people offer major lessons, others minor. They are all here to offer a lesson. The lesson is always the same, to remove the fears and judgments that are in the way of our loving each person unconditionally. Each person is in our life as a blessing, though this may not be immediately apparent. If we will allow unconditional, nonjudgmental love to enter the relationship, even if only briefly, a change will occur and the relationship will alter in an unforeseen way that will offer us growth and development. We will have learned the intended lesson and will be free of the negative ties of the relationship.

CHAPTER 1

Working Together Learning Together

Human relationships are why we are here. Through them we grow and awaken. Our purpose here, in this school called earth, is to remove all the fears that block our true nature, love, from emerging and expressing itself. We accomplish this through our interactions with others. Though this may be somewhat more obvious in our family and social relationships, this is no less true for the relationships in our worklives. Nor are these work relationships any less important to our learning process. No one is in our lives by accident. Though relationships take many forms, each comes with the same lesson, to teach and learn love, for that is what we are.

Forgiveness is the key to our growth and happiness, and judgment and resentment, of ourselves or others, is the source of our pain. Relationships that we enjoy and that offer us little stress tend to trigger fewer of our fears than those that trouble and upset us. This is as it should be. Our loving relationships are no less important to our growth but we are already successfully learning our lesson in these.

That is why they are loving and clear. Our troubling relationships are those that trigger our fears and judgments, thereby giving us the opportunity to understand and release them.

Our troubling relationships need only one adjustment to resolve them. This is forgiveness. This forgiveness is not the traditional understanding of the term, where we acknowledge that someone has treated us unfairly and that we will grant them reprieve from retribution or revenge. Real forgiveness means to have understood that we were never unfairly treated in the first place. It means to bring truth and clarity to the relationship by remembering that there are only two emotions, love and fear. Correspondingly, there are only two forms of behavior, extending love or asking for love. Fearful and attacking behavior that we perceive as unfair treatment, is simply an asking for love in a convoluted form. The appropriate response to someone asking us for love is to offer them love. This is true forgiveness, a remembrance and awareness of who we really are, beings of love shrouded in judgment and fear. This will serve to help the other person remember as well. This allows the miracle to enter the relationship and healing to occur.

Each one of us has relationships that continue to upset us and rob us of our peace of mind. Usually, we blame the other person for this, and occasionally, we blame ourselves. Our world view will decide whether we control these situations or whether they control us. If our view of the Universe is that it operates in a random pattern, then we will not view the situations or people in our lives as being there for a reason. We will feel that we are either lucky or unlucky to encounter different situations and people. This can lead to a sense of helplessness and a feeling that we are out of control of our lives. People seem to wander in and out of our lives. Some seem to be a blessing, others a curse, and yet others unimportant and of little consequence to us. We tend to view others in regard to how they fulfill or frustrate our needs and goals. This view of the Universe represents a basic misunderstanding. It views us as the effect, not the cause, of the relationships and situations in our lives. With this view of the Universe, it is easy to perceive ourselves as victims.

Another view of relationships, one that is not so obvious yet may be the most common, perceives the Universe as one created by a punitive God. Painful relationships are then interpreted accordingly. They are both proof and punishment of some inherent flaw or "sin" within ourselves or another. The pain in the relationship is just due for the sins we, or they, have committed (unloving acts, dishonesty, inattentiveness, etc.). The pain involved, and the pain we desire to cause in retribution, is the punishment for the "sin." We (or they) deserve it. We have mistakenly interpreted the pain as an end instead of a means, a justification for attack rather than a prompting to forgiveness.

There is another view of the Universe that places us as the creator (actually, the cocreator) of our Universe. We are the cause, not the effect, of the situations in our lives. Since there are only errors, not sins, we are in need of correcting the errors, rather than blaming or condemning ourselves for the painful situations. If we begin to understand that the people in our lives are there for only one reason, so that we may learn and teach love through our interactions with them, we have made a major step towards the reinterpretation of our own Universe. We can begin to feel that we really do have control of our lives and that we have called each person and situation into our life with a similar goal. When any situation occurs that tends to upset us, we can ask ourselves, "What is the lesson here?" The true answer is always the same. The relationship's function is to teach us to release our fears, of not being loved or being unlovable, and to love ourselves and the other person unconditionally.

Our most upsetting relationships offer us our greatest opportunities.

This does not mean that we must learn to like the other person or to accept the way they behave. We need to evaluate and discern their *behavior* instead of judging them as people. Nor does it mean that we must remain in a relationship with them. It only means that we are able to view them as beings worthy of our unconditional love, though we find their behavior unappealing and objectionable. Remembering that we are always either extending or seeking love, we are also able to

3

see that this type of behavior is their painful way of asking for love. Everyone is worthy of our love because everyone, like us, is suffering from temporary amnesia. We have forgotten we were created in love and are love, and it is only due to this amnesia that our fearful behavior manifests itself. When we have remembered this about our fellow human beings, especially those that upset us, we will have remembered this about ourselves.

Our most upsetting relationships offer us our greatest opportunities for growth since they trigger our deepest fears. Those relationships are symbols of unrest in our mind. If we are having problems in our worklife with an employee or employer, a client or customer, the most common response is to blame the other person and seek avenues of revenge, escape, or avoidance. Or we may blame ourselves and seek revenge through guilt. However, an alternative view is to realize that we have created this situation and to seek out the blocks we may have to loving (though not always liking or enjoying) the other person. Upsetting relationships or interactions reflect our fears back to us.

The fact that the person has upset us is testimony that we are responding fearfully. They have triggered some fear that we have not yet confronted or resolved. In truth, it is our fear that has caused us to create someone in our lives that will treat us in this manner. They are simply reflecting our fears back to us, as we are to them. Herein lies the blessing and gift of the relationship. It has offered us the opportunity to expose and release this fear. We can begin to see that the fear is not valid; rather, it is inappropriate. We need the blessing as much as the other person needs the blessing of our forgiveness. Otherwise we all remain locked into our illusions of anger and resentment.

If an employer treats us disrespectfully, this triggers a fear that we are unlovable, undervalued, incompetent, or in some other way flawed. If a co-worker never values our opinions or judgments, perhaps they are reflecting our fear that our opinions are of little value. If a customer treats us in a hostile manner, they may be reflecting our fear that we are deserving of little respect. At first, it may seem that their behavior is proof that our fear is valid. However, just the opposite is true. Their behavior is an opportunity, a blessing, that exposes our fear to us so that we may see it is not real. As soon as we have done this and released the fear, their behavior and/or our relationship with them will change.

Once we perceive that this fearful pattern exists, anger often emerges: anger at ourselves for creating the pattern and at the other person for participating in and supporting the pattern. However, we can avoid any damage done by reacting from anger by realizing that they are as trapped in the pattern by their fears as we are and would also like to be free, even if they are not consciously aware of it. Since we have uncovered it first, we can help lead them out of it. As long as the anger persists it is a symptom that though the fear may have been uncovered, it is not yet resolved. When it is, we will feel peace, not anger.

The opportunity for peace and forgiveness is always open to us.

It is easy to perceive relationships in our workplace as important only in regards to our work, not to our personal growth. It would seem that we are brought together to work and that is the extent of our relationship. In truth, these relationships are no different than those in our personal life in regard to their purpose and to the impact they have on our growth.

The same fears that are at work in our personal lives influence us in our workplace. People are brought together in both our work and personal lives as part of our life tapestry, woven from the individual threads of each relationship. In each relationship we are given the same opportunity to teach and learn either love or fear, to offer love and forgiveness or fear and illusion.

Many of us spend as much of our waking lives in our workplace as in our homes. This allows us the opportunity to relate with many different people outside our nuclear family. Unlike our personal relationships, where we often "choose" the people we relate with and have some degree of control about their participation in our lives, our work "family" seems to be chosen for us and at random. Because of this, we may not feel as responsible to keep these relationships clear and loving. Again, an adjustment of this view is needed. All our relationships, whether they are in our home, workplace, or anywhere else, are of equal importance. We are here to awaken and remind each other of our goal of love.

When anyone suggests that maybe we should consider loving a person we are in conflict with, a lot of resistance will surface. This resistance encourages us to rationalize why we cannot or do not want to cease our anger and attack on another and begin to love them. Allowing ourselves to open our hearts and love someone we are in conflict with does not necessarily mean we are committed to remain physically or emotionally in the relationship. In fact, the opposite is true. By keeping our heart closed to the other person and not resolving our feelings of anger and hostility, even if it is only expressed as mild irritation, we are not completing our assigned lesson with them. The relationship has become rigid and stuck and we are not allowing resolution and healing so that we might move on, physically and/or emotionally. Even if we never see the person again or if they are dead, we are stuck and bound in that relationship until we have resolved all our unloving feelings.

Forgiving another does not mean allowing their fearful and upsetting behavior to continue. Forgiving means only that we have pierced the illusion of the fearful behavior and understood it as a request for love. In offering them the love they have sought we may also decide that we do not want to allow their offensive behavior to continue and that we must confront them. The difference now, is that we do so from an awareness of love and understanding, not judgment and anger. By making this essential shift in our minds, our subsequent actions, for which inner guidance will be offered, will not only alter their behavior but offer them love and healing as well. Though their initial or outward response may be anger, indignation, or judgment, your love and forgiveness has created the miracle, and its effects, though sometimes unobservable, are sure.

Often, when we are in an upsetting relationship with someone in any area of our lives, we consider leaving the relationship (by divorce, quitting, firing, etc.). One fear we have is that, should we resolve our negative feelings towards this person, it will mean that we are destined to remain in this relationship. This is not necessarily the case. We may find that even though we are able to perceive the person differently and understand that their upsetting or attacking behavior is a convoluted way of asking for love, we still may desire to remove ourselves from a close relationship with them. However, resolving our bitterness and releasing our desire to attack, no matter how much we may feel these emotions are justified, allows resolution to enter the relationship, at least for those who are able to make the transition to love. We will have learned the lesson that that relationship was meant to teach us, to teach and learn love. We are in many ways now "free" from the fears and conflict that were holding us in this relationship.

The other person may not resolve their own angry feelings. It is not necessary that they do for us to complete *our* relationship with them. It is not even necessary that they be present in our lives or even alive, for forgiveness and peace to enter. The opportunity for peace and forgiveness is always open to us, no matter how great the perceived injustice, how long the conflict, or how distant the person. An ancient bitterness can always become a present love. A loving God could not condemn his children to a lifetime of unresolved relationships.

Often we feel that we cannot change a painful relationship if the other person does not want it to change as well. This fear is quite understandable since we have been taught that it takes two to make a conflict, and therefore assume that it takes two to resolve one. However, it only takes one to end the conflict—for that person. Peace can enter a relationship, at least for the person who has brought it from illusion to truth, from conflict to forgiveness. Though we do not have control over, or responsibility for, another person's feelings and actions towards us, we do have both control and responsibility for how we choose to react towards their thoughts, feelings, and actions. By altering and eventually mastering our own thoughts and feelings in the relationship in order to extend love, we can then regain control over the effect the relationship has on us. We allowed the relationship to control us by not controlling our thoughts and emotions and thereby, we can reverse the process. In doing so, we also give the other person greater freedom to truly be who they are.

When forgiveness enters a relationship, a path will be made clear to us that is in our own best interest. If one possible path is to curtail or end the relationship, physically and/or emotionally, this will be open to us and we can freely choose it. If there seems to be no path open to leave the relationship we may still have yet more to learn through it or we may find that we can continue in the relationship but without the inner conflict and struggle we experienced before.

If we view a particular relationship as beyond our control and one in which we are being unfairly treated, we will feel powerless to change it. This will lead to depression and anger. If, however, we begin to understand that we are actually creating all the relationships and situations in our lives, we will also understand that we have complete control over how we react to them. Our emotions no longer control us. In a relationship that is causing us upset, whether it be major or minor upset or a major or minor relationship, we need to first ask ourselves why we are creating this relationship. Blaming either ourselves or others is usually our first response, and understandably so, given a perception of the Universe as random or punitive. We tend to see ourselves as a victim and hence, will blame the other person, or as emotionally "flawed" and therefore will blame ourselves (through guilt). We usually feel a blend of these two feelings.

However, eventually we need to understand that blame and guilt are never appropriate, even though they appear reasonable and justified from the world's point of view. Blame infers guilt which infers sin which demands punishment. Our fears may have caused us and others to make mistakes that need correcting, but we have not sinned and do not need punishment.

No one is able to upset us unless we allow them.

Another major resistance to forgiveness is the feeling that we are justified in seeking retribution and revenge for the harm done to us. This represents a basic fallacy in the understanding of the true nature of human behavior. If revenge is what we want, at some level we have decided that we were attacked without justification and therefore the other person must experience pain equal to or greater than what they inflicted on us. We think they have sinned and therefore must be punished. If we feel that way about others, we feel that way about ourselves, knowing that we are not perfect either. We feel that we too have sinned and therefore must be punished. If we believe in God, we will view Him as a God who records our sins and doles out our appropriate punishments. When we do this, we are creating God in *our* image instead of remembering we are made in *His* image, which is one of unconditional love. This type of thinking leads to guilt and anger towards ourselves and others. If we honestly dissect our anger, we will find that it is an attempt to create guilt in others or ourselves.

An honest questioning allows us to see that we are never upset for the reasons we think (*Course*, workbook, p. 8). We are not upset because we feel attacked or unfairly treated by someone, but rather, because they are touching some fear that we have, usually in regard to our own sense of self-worth. No one is able to upset us unless we allow them. We are usually upset because we view someone's upsetting behavior as either an unjustified or justified attack. No attack is justified because all offensive behavior is in reality an asking for love. And no response to a person's asking for love is appropriate but to give them love.

We can correct our perceptions by beginning to view these forms of attack, by ourselves and others, not as sins demanding punishment, but rather as errors needing correction and as distorted pleas for love (*Course*, text, p. 377). We were once told to take an eye for an eye and a tooth for a tooth, implying revenge. This message has been misunderstood. What we were actually being told was to take no greater revenge or retribution than the damage that was inflicted upon us. If we lost an eye, take only an eye, not two eyes. It was a warning not to overreact. This was all we could understand and accept at the time. As the species grew and began to learn at a more advanced level, we were told not to demand equal retribution but rather to love our enemies and bless those that harm us. We have now grown able to understand the next level of forgiveness, that there is nothing to forgive because we have never been unjustly treated. Someone was sent into our life with a goal to learn and asked for our love in a distorted and convoluted manner, which we mistakenly perceived as unjust treatment or obnoxious behavior. This asking provides us with the opportunity to give them the love they are asking for (forgiveness). We are in need of the blessing as much as they. If we are able to view all unloving actions, both by ourselves and those directed towards us by others, as convoluted ways of asking for love, we will understand the appropriate response is always to give love. What would you offer to a person who asked you for love but love? We can then begin to create ourselves in the image of our Creator, who never forgives because He never condemns (*Course,* workbook, p. 73).

Perhaps there is someone in our worklife who continues to treat us in an unloving and hostile manner. They seem always to be attacking us though our actions do not seem to justify attack. The truth is, they are attacking us because they do not love themselves or feel themselves to be unworthy of love. People who love themselves and who feel they are worthy of the love and respect of others, do not treat people unlovingly. If we can quiet our anger and our judgment, we will be able to see a desperate asking for love in that person's attack on us. The appropriate response to this is to offer love in return. It is what we are taught when we are asked to love our enemies. We do not need to be reminded to love our friends or those who love us, because this is easy to do. Loving our enemies means to love those that attack us and treat us unlovingly. Though understanding and forgiveness may seem very difficult to achieve, it is much less difficult than living with the unresolved anger and conflict that constantly robs us of our peace of mind. To quote an old saying, "Resentment does more damage to the vessel in which it is stored, than to the object on which it is poured." Do we want revenge and resentment or peace and happiness? We cannot have both.

There is a ripple effect to our genuine act of forgiveness and these ripples will usually not be observable to us. Everyone witnessing real forgiveness is touched and inspired by it and encouraged to do likewise in their own relationships. By forgiving and loving those whom we perceive to have treated us unjustly and unlovingly, we are teaching love to all those who are aware of the situation. By attacking in "justifiable" revenge, however much we may feel it to be justified, we are teaching fear. When our attacks are victorious and we have defeated the other person, everyone on our side will agree that the offending party deserved the painful defeat. In this case, we are teaching each other fear and attack. If we teach fear we will remain fearful. If we teach love we will know peace.

Here are two dramatic examples of people's ability to respond with love and forgiveness in the face of intense personal attack. The first is well known, the second less so. Sometime after the death of his son, Dr. Martin Luther King, Jr., Dr. King, Sr. was on the pulpit during a service at his church, the Ebenezer Baptist Church in Atlanta. A person in the crowd fired shots at Dr. King but missed, instead striking and killing his wife of many years. As Dr. King held his beloved, dying wife in his arms, his response to her murderer was that we must offer him love and forgiveness, not hate and condemnation.

Earlier in his life, Dr. King, Sr. had not always been known for such a capacity to forgive. Surely his firsthand observations of his son's ability to do this, even after repeated personal and physical assaults, had caused this transformation in him. On the eve of his own assassination, Dr. King, Jr. demonstrated this clarity in a statement he made. He spoke to a crowd saying his aides had begged him not to come to Memphis because of threats to his life by "some of my sick white brothers." This one statement is testimony that he had pierced the illusion and was seeing them clearly. He understood that these people represented "some," not all, that they were "sick," not evil, and that even they were his "brothers." Dr. King, Sr. had watched his son teach love, no matter what the circumstances, and in doing so he had also learned it. In his action as his wife lay dying, he had the opportunity to teach this to us all.

If we teach fear we will remain fearful. If we teach love we will know peace.

It is all too easy to dismiss this degree of love and forgiveness as something appropriate for larger than life figures such as the Kings, but not for everyday people like ourselves. The following example shows that this degree of understanding and clarity of response is available to everyone. The event took place in a midwestern city several years ago. A young girl was murdered by a teenage boy who lived in the neighborhood. The neighbors and the city were outraged. The boy was arrested and his family was under siege in their home from angry citizens, who wondered what kind of parents could raise such a child.

Soon after the murder, the parents of the young girl called a news conference. Everyone expected anger and hostility to be justifiably aimed at the boy's parents. To everyone's amazement, the boy's parents appeared at their side at the conference. The girl's parents told the community that they had forgiven the boy and his family and asked everyone to do the same so that no greater pain would be heaped onto this tragic situation.

These acts of love and forgiveness affected thousands, perhaps millions of people as the press reports carried their stories. The ripples continue to affect everyone who hears of them, as it has just done to you. Many of the effects of these miracles were not observable or apparent to the people creating them. However, they remind us that there exists a higher way to react to unjustified attacks, which are in reality convoluted forms of asking for love. They remind us that if people are capable of forgiving the murder of their loved ones, then we can be capable of forgiving anyone. This was the message of the crucifixion. That forgiveness is possible and appropriate, even after betrayal, desertion, and even murder.

Competition / Cooperation

The business world has been based on the concept of competition. There is little in a competitive perception that encourages or nurtures love and forgiveness. Competition will never allow us to view other people correctly. They must always be viewed as separate from us, as someone to be defeated or conquered, as someone to be better than, or as a threat to our desired goals. Competition has been mistakenly acknowledged as a builder of character and the most powerful motivator in the workplace. However, the real motivator that underlies competition is often fear—fear of losing, fear of not being as good as someone else, fear of being dominated, fear of someone taking something from us. Fear, and therefore competition, is indeed a powerful human motivator but it is neither the best nor the healthiest.

As has been mentioned before, there are two basic emotions, love and fear, and therefore only two possible motivators (*Course*, text, p. 230). Of these two, love is the more powerful, being based on who we really are, whereas fear is based on fearful illusions of who we are.

Though competition may sometimes bring out the best in certain services and products, it may bring out the worst in people. Love, as a motivator for human action, does no emotional damage to those involved.

Inherent in the competitive concept of someone winning is someone losing. It is a win-lose relationship, not a win-win one. As a society, we have come to accept competition as a necessity of life and even to praise it as a much desired condition. We have continued to justify its existence by pointing to the winners and applauding their accomplishments. However, several things have been overlooked in this analysis. First, we avoid looking at the effect competition has on the larger group of its participants, the losers. To the people who feel they have lost in a competition, hurt feelings, a sense of lack of self-

Though competition may sometimes bring out the best in certain services and products, it may bring out the worst in people.

worth or even self-condemnation, can follow. This can lead to anger and depression. The loser may be propelled to try even harder, but this is usually fueled by the anger and fear created by the previous losses. Enough of these losses, often beginning in early childhood, can cause someone to see themselves as a loser in life and not as worthy as others.

It would be easy to believe that only the "losers" are negatively affected by a competitive system, but this is not the case. Winning perpetuates illusions. It can make people feel superior to their peers and friends. This perpetuates the illusion that we are all separate, rather than the truth that we are all one, connected and equal. It can lead to the glorification and fixation of the ego and the intoxication with our own successes. It can cause us to view those around us not as people to be enjoyed and loved, but as opponents to be defeated. A competitive system does not encourage helping or nurturing but rather defeating and overpowering.

Any system which creates self-condemnation or an illusion of superiority and separation in its participants, and which includes fear, anger, shame, and a desire to defeat others as its motivators, is one that will do extensive emotional damage to all involved, both winners and losers. In the process, it will often poison the relationships of those involved in the system. Can anyone be considered a winner if their prize is a greater sense of separation and alienation and a false sense of superiority over his or her peers? Surely a system that builds one person's self-esteem through fear, shame, and at the cost of another's, is insane. God has not condemned His children to do their best at the expense of others.

Another factor in competition is that it uses the fear of losing, and the subsequent sense of shame, as a motivator. It trains us to believe that if we do not defeat enough of our competitors, we are less than them and therefore unworthy. We may have even come to falsely believe that our value as a person is in accordance to our "ranking" among others, that the more people we can surpass, the better we are. The fear that we, as well as others, may perceive ourselves to be unworthy in any endeavor, may compel us to work harder and "do better" but there is a heavy price to pay for this fear-based motivation.

Even with all its drawbacks we have come to believe that without intense competition, people will not strive to do their best and accomplishments will diminish. This is understandable but not valid. Management by fear is prevalent in today's workplace. There is a natural resistance to abandon a system that has been working, even if the cost of its success is great. However, there is a clearer and more powerful inspiration for human action. Love and cooperation can replace fear and competition as human motivators and the subsequent results will reflect a love-based stimulus as opposed to a fear-based one. These results, these achievements, will be inherently different due to the fact that their emotional source and inspiration comes from love, the exact opposite of fear. Creations always directly reflect the consciousness of their creator. By changing this consciousness from fear to love you can vastly alter the resulting creations. Everything "created" naturally through love will affect those involved quite differently than things "made" through fear.

It is possible to be motivated to achieve through a deep assurance of our inherent self-worth, rather than through a false fear of its lack. As we begin to understand that our self-worth is our birthright, we will stop seeking our worth through things outside ourselves, including our comparative ranking with other individuals. It is only our mistaken lack of self-worth that has caused us to seek it there. As we truly begin to love ourselves, and begin to remember that we are created by a totally loving Creator, in His image, the underlying inspiration for our activity will have undergone a deep and indelible change. When this shift is begun, the effect on our lives and our achievements is profound.

Behavior and achievements inspired and motivated by our self-love and our understanding of our divine origin and nature will affect all those involved only to their benefit, even if this involves a certain amount of pain. There will be no "losers," only "winners." It is truly a win-win situation. Love does not require some losers in order that others may win. By its nature, it will serve to remind others of their own self-worth, not of their own self-lack. Motivated by our understanding of our true nature, we desire not to defeat others but to assist others in reestablishing their awareness of their own self-worth. We will not be tempted to gloat over our achievements; we will be less inclined to view them as the accomplishments of our individual egos but rather the natural outcome of a Universal Spirit working through us. These love-based achievements will have a transformational and positive effect on those involved, whereas fear-based achievements will tend to further fixate and solidify fears. We will be teaching love not fear.

Achievements that are the results of our ego desires, which so many of our existing achievements are, will always involve a degree of stress and strain, often to the degree that they may damage our bodies in the process. In addition to a negative effect on the body, relationships may suffer as well as the ego drives take their toll. Competition does not support friendship or foster true caring between people. Achievements resulting from cooperation, high self-esteem, and a sense of mission will not have these damaging effects.

Every day new medical, technical, and scientific breakthroughs are announced. Many of these are the valuable results of an all-out effort to get to the marketplace before a competitor. How much less energy would have been needed and less time required had all the parties cooperated instead of competed? In business, we often do things that are inherently counterproductive to our corporate or stated goals, but which may increase our personal position within the workplace. How much more could a business produce if the environment was one of cooperation instead of competition? A competitive system is inefficient. Why not avoid doing damage in the pursuit of our goals if this is possible?

Competition does work and its results can be of value, but it is an archaic and inefficient system at best and a destructive and vicious one at its worst. Until now though, it has been the best system we have known. It has fueled the industrial revolution and, given our previous levels of awareness, was an appropriate step on the path towards cooperation. However, for the coming times it will need to be replaced by a system of cooperation at all levels. We must teach this to our children as well as practice it in our homes and workplaces. The coming environmental emergencies and the need to lower humankind's competitive, aggressive emotions so as to avert a nuclear holocaust, demand that we switch from a fear-based competitive system to a love-based cooperative one. The human species must work together to continue its life on the planet.

Cooperation encourages a view of others as equals and helpers in our goals. It nurtures a sense of friendship, love, and support. It brings people together in the accomplishment of a task, rather than pitting them against each other. It provides for a "win-win" scenario, thereby freeing the losers from a sense of inadequacy and the winners from a sense of superiority and arrogance. It allows truth to enter the situation, the truth that we are all brothers and sisters whose function it is to assist each other with love and support.

In a certain respect, competition does have its place in a cooperative world. In this world, we compete to do our best, not to be the best. We compete against or challenge our own limits, with little need to compare our results to those of others. This type of competition must also be based in love and high self-esteem. We must come from a point of view that we already have an inherent self-worth; in challenging of our limits we can acquire even greater freedom and joy. We are peacefully pushing ourselves, not to avoid the pain of failure or disapproval, but to experience the joys and blessings of extending our limits. This type of motivation is healthy and will not cause damage as it encourages balance and compassion in its pursuit of its goals.

When we pursue our goals free of much of the stress and strain that fear-based emotions cause, we are much more effective. We are balanced and centered, not fatigued and worried. Choosing fear as a motivator will deplete us. From this depleted position we will make poor choices and have less energy available to understand the effect our actions may be having on those around us.

From a balanced position, our faculties are at their best and our vision is clearest. Because of this, our decision making can be the most effective, allowing us to choose the best of all possible alternatives available to us. We will work better and smarter instead of harder.

The human species must work together to continue its life on the planet.

Another phenomena occurs when we switch to a motivational basis of love and trust. We begin to perceive and sense not only what we can accomplish but also what we are being guided to accomplish. We begin to discern our mission. We can begin to pursue goals that include within them the good of all involved. As we do this we are aligning with our life purpose, to teach and learn love. When this begins to happen, something else "miraculous" occurs. All types of conditions, situations, and opportunities in our physical world, in our workplace, begin to materialize to support these clearer goals. This assistance will often appear as totally unpredictable and may be regarded as simply good luck or coincidence. Goals will become more easily attained than expected and at times may even seem effortless.

What is occurring is not good luck but miracles. Miracles are not supernatural. In fact, when they are not occurring, something is unnatural (*Course*, text, p. 1). They occur naturally as the peaceful creation of any act based on love and trust. We can choose to painfully and stressfully "make" things happen with the force of our human will and the desires of our ego. Or we can choose to "create" and peacefully achieve—guided and assisted by our divine nature—inspired outcomes for the good of all involved.

> **L**isted below are commonly
> accepted principles and their underlying
> fears. Score yourself on a scale from 1 to
> 10 to see how your present thoughts
> and emotions are formed by these
> principles and fears.

Accepted Principles

1 A person's presence in my life represents a blessing, a curse, or a random turning of the Universe. _____

2 There is nothing for me to learn in an upsetting relationship. It is just something I would like to see end. _____

3 There is no way to get an upsetting relationship to change, especially if the other person does not want it to change. I must either accept it as it is or leave the relationship. _____

4 Due to the nature of the relationship, i.e., boss/employee, client/contractor, wife/husband, this is the best I can expect in this type of relationship. _____

5 The other person is at fault and wrong in the way they are treating me and I am right. This justifies my attacking them (verbally and/or emotionally). _____

6 My life would be better and I would be happier if people would stop doing the things that upset me. _____

7 I do not deserve greater respect, love, or considerate treatment. _____

8 People that upset me are often not capable of greater respect, love, or considerate treatment. _____

Fears Underlying Accepted Principles

1 The Universe operates randomly and I fear I have little or no control over the things and relationships that often affect my life. _____

2 When things or people cause me pain, stress, discomfort, or anxiety, I am in a negative situation that needs to be avoided or endured. There is no positive value to these people or situations. _____

3 I fear things or people cause me pain, stress, anxiety, and discomfort because the Universe (or God) operates on punitive principles and I am being punished for past impure thoughts, feelings, or actions. _____

4 I fear that many relationships that are upsetting and stressful cannot be changed. They must just be endured or avoided. _____

Fears Regarding Forgiving

5 If I attempt to correct this relationship by "forgiving" perceived transgressions against me, I fear I am being weak. It is the other person, the "transgressor," that should ask for forgiveness before I grant it. _____

6 I fear that if I "forgive" this person, their negative behavior towards me will continue and perhaps heighten. _____

7 I fear that if I "forgive" this person, there will never be any retribution or payment for their "sins" against me. _____

8 I fear that if I "forgive" this person, it may mean that I must remain physically and/or emotionally in the relationship. _____

9 I fear that if I "forgive" this person, it may appear to them and others that they were "right" and I was "wrong." _____

Given that our purpose here always involves the teaching and learning of love, we can trust that any work that is truly meant for us will allow us the time and energy to advance this goal at home. Balance between our home and worklives is not only possible but essential for us in order to accomplish our mission.

CHAPTER 2

The Family As Balance

Perhaps nowhere in our modern culture is the imbalance in our lives more obvious and more damaging than in our family lives. Our family represents the most important relationships of our lives. Our lives are given real value by our relationships with people, not by our relationships with our possessions, our accomplishments, or our careers. In recent years, especially with women entering the work force in such numbers the value placed on the family and child rearing has changed. More and more, we have placed things and accomplishments above people. We have forgotten why we are here.

Our accomplishments and our possessions are valuable only when they serve as a vehicle to enhance our relationship with ourselves and other people. Their true purpose is to provide a context in which relationships, and therefore love, can grow. Accomplishments and possessions have no intrinsic value in and of themselves. Their value is established by the effect they have on the people involved with them. However, in this society, based so heavily on commerce, we often forget this and place a value on things separate from the manner in which they affect us and those with whom we are involved.

Some of this country's greatest assets are its wealth, its high level of commercial efficiency and success, and its tremendous abundance. These are also its greatest liabilities. We have come to praise and honor our possessions, our wealth, and our achievements. We have made them our gods. We have come to see the physical body as an end in itself, not a means. It is perceived as a pleasure-getting tool to be used to get what we desire. In "reality," it is a learning and communication vehicle to be used for our awakening.

Our lives are given real values by our relationships with people.

Many people have been viewed as highly successful by the outside world, only to be failures in, and to, their families. In fact, we have often come to think that success in both home and work may be unlikely, if not impossible. The syndrome is one of public success combined with private "failure" and emptiness. This sense of failure in our family lives often propels us to spend more and more energy and time at our work, where our successes are measurable and acknowledged. For single people their work can become a substitute for love and affection. This may indicate that we have forgotten why we are here, to learn and teach love.

We have replaced this purpose with the belief that we are here to accomplish, possess, glorify our individual egos, and to satisfy our desires. If that is why we are here, then having acquired this should lead us to joy and peace of mind, once we have accomplished our task. However, an in-depth look at the inner lives of some of our most "successful" people often reflects not peace and joy, but confusion and anguish.

There are lessons that can be learned (and taught) in the intimacy of the family unit that may be difficult to learn elsewhere. Our families are usually not as concerned with our business success and accomplishments as they are with our success as a human being: as a father, a mother, or a spouse. These successes are measured by our simple, everyday interactions with our family members. They are measured by the way we care for, and are attentive to, those close around us. They are measured by the way we are able to place the interests of others equal to or above our own.

In many ways, the value we place on different areas of our lives is directly associated with the amount of time and attention we spend on them. The more we value something, the more time and attention we offer it. We then have to ask what message we are sending to our children, spouses, family members, and friends when we spend fifty, sixty, or seventy hours a week in our worklives and only a few hours a week with them. No matter how much we may feel we love them, it sends the message that we value them far less than our careers and herein lies the damage that we do. It may be that our fears of failing in our careers and businesses are greater than our fears of failing in our family life. We really do not need to operate from fear of failure in either. Often, we may physically be at home but our thoughts may still be at work. We are physically present but emotionally absent. We need to learn the balance of not bringing our work to our home or our home to our work.

Children (and other family members) who observe their parents in a dedicated pursuit of greater achievements and possessions and yet daily feel the pain of parents who seldom seem to have the time, energy, or patience to really be with them, begin to feel of little value. That is the message we as parents send to them. "I'm busy with my work. I do not have time to fix your meal, go to your games, be with you when you need me. I'm tired. I can't play with you now. I need to make more money, accomplish more, own more things. I'm sorry. My work is important and gets my full attention. You are less important and get attention when I can give it." We may say it to them many times every week, in many unspoken ways. (Often we are saying the same thing to our mates and friends.) They hear it many times every week. In time they begin to feel they are not so important. They begin to feel physically provided for but emotionally abandoned. In time, they may begin to stop communicating, develop low self-esteem, stop trying in school, act obnoxious, and / or abuse drugs, alcohol, food, or sex. When you no longer value yourself, all forms of self-destructive behavior begin to arise. They do not value who they are because they were not valued *enough* by their parents or caregivers. We have become lost in the insane value system of our culture.

Our modern business community has placed little respect on the role of families in the creation of a balanced and healthy life. Though this is now slowly changing, it is for the most part still true. Little concern is given to the trauma imposed on the family by requiring that people continue to relocate to pursue their careers. Little effort is made to assist employees in keeping their workweeks within a reasonable range so that they have the needed time to properly handle the other important areas of their lives. Companies seldom encourage their people to take time away from their offices to be available for family events, especially the ones that we all too quickly term "unimportant." The hero of the business community is the dedicated worker who is at the office at 7:00 A.M. and leaves at 7:00 P.M., takes work home, and commits at least one weekend day to the job.

Workaholism has become society's only acceptable addiction. This acceptability allows us to deny the damage the addiction does both to the addict and their family. We have come to see the number of hours a person works as a sign of their commitment to their jobs or business. In reality, long hours are only a sign of the degree to which they are avoiding other areas of their lives. It is a sign of misplaced priorities, of a life out-of-balance. (In Japan this concept has been carried to an extreme and they actually have a name, *karoshi*, for a death that occurs by being burnt-out from work. The Japanese work longer hours than anyone in the developed world.)

We have come to believe that success in our business life is the indication of our success as a person. We may remember all the "love" and attention we received from parents, teachers, and peers when we accomplished something everyone thought was "good" (good grades, good performance at sports, good reports, etc.). We often pass this "busyness" and need to achieve on to our children by enrolling them in an endless number of outside classes and activities. This can rob a child of one of the great gifts of childhood—unstructured play time. We have come to understand that in this world people often like us more for what we do, rather than who we are. The pursuit of seeking people's esteem through our accomplishments often dominates our lives and is part of the reason we allow our lives to get out-of-balance. It is our fear-based emotions that have created a painful life-situation.

24

If we peel the fears back one more layer we will see that if we truly loved ourselves, the esteem of others would not be of such importance that we would allow this to happen. If we truly understood that our worth is already established by our Creator and our true nature—love—and not by our status, accomplishments, or possessions, imbalance would be impossible.

If we attempt to establish our self-worth, both to ourselves and to others, by our achievements and/or financial status, this will always lead to serious imbalance. The pursuit of accomplishments and money will throw our lives off-center. Even if we reach the needed level of accomplishments or wealth, we will find the victory to be hollow and will not grant us the peace of mind we had struggled and hoped for. It may give us a temporary sense of satisfaction or a thrill of accomplishment or ownership, but it cannot grant real and lasting peace. This peace can only be found as we free ourselves from our fears (not by placating them) to the point that they do not warp our vision and perception. With clearer vision, we will see that we have always been of great value. We are beings that are sent by our Creator, in his image, to produce miracles through the teaching and learning of love. Our worth was and is our birthright. No accomplishments or possessions can either enhance or diminish this worth. Indeed, our business accomplishments and our possessions are just trinkets compared to the real value we possess.

Workaholism has become society's only acceptable addiction.

Our children need to be seen as our greatest teachers. The task of raising them to be happy, loving individuals is the most important task we will ever be given. In this work lies the future of the species. This task is of great importance both to ourselves and our children. We need to reverse our decisions to continually sacrifice the things that matter most on the altar of the things that matter least.

In addition to being our greatest teachers, children are also our greatest gifts, for many reasons, one of which is that they provide us the opportunity to rebalance ourselves as adults (a stage at which most of us have lost this natural balance). By asking ourselves what our children need to be happy, well-adjusted individuals, we will discover that by providing them these needs, we ourselves will become happier and better adjusted. Their needs are simple, just as ours can be.

Children do not care what sale we have just made, what promotion has been earned, what the bottom line is, or how much money is in the bank. In their earliest years they are only concerned with the relationships of the people around them. If they are loved and major fears are not transferred to them, they will remain happy and free. They are getting everything they need. If these primary relationships are not loving or loving yet heavily burdened by pain due to inattention, the child will begin to develop fears. We may love our children a great deal and yet not be giving them the time and attention they need. We may bring many fears to the relationship. These fears include a fear that they will be injured; that we are not parenting correctly; that we are not spending quality and/or quantity time with them; or that they are not growing, acting, or succeeding as we think they should. To the degree we bring our fears into our relationship with them, is the degree to which we will teach them fear, not love.

In their early years children feel most secure in a mundane, unexciting environment. This is often the environment many of us find the hardest to accept. We are seeking the next high, the next party or trip, the next major accomplishment, the next purchase. We are losing touch with the value of everyday normal life, spending periods of quantity *and* quality time with the ones we love. Yet it is just this type of environment that is most conducive to raising well-adjusted children and parents. What is best for the youngest of the species is probably best for us all.

We must also free ourselves from the illusion that we need to be remarkable or do remarkable things. Just as one great meal will not satisfy our hunger forever, so one great accomplishment will not satisfy our search for meaning and value in our lives forever. It is our everyday interactions, both large and small, that create meaning in our lives. Each moment of each day is remarkable as it offers an opportunity to create miracles by our love.

If we begin to honor our roles as parents and begin to place the needs of our children equal to or above our own, many benefits occur for us and our lives begin to regain their equilibrium. These benefits show how children are our best teachers. Childrens' needs in many ways reflect human qualities of enduring and mature values. An intelligent observation of children shows that what they need is love, affection, time, understanding, someone to listen to them, play, fun, friends, rest and relaxation, protection against stress and negativity, consistency in day-to-day life, and peace and calm in the home. An intelligent observation of what we need when we are out-of-balance will reflect the exact same list of needs.

Our children need to be seen as our greatest teachers.

This one shift, to intelligently determine the needs of our children and then set up the circumstances whereby these needs can be met, will cause changes in our own lives that will bring us back into balance. We will give them more of our time and attention, we will be home more, we will create a peaceful and calm home by becoming more peaceful ourselves, we will not always be willing to place the needs of children and family second to the needs of our work.

Children truly are our greatest gift as well as our greatest teachers. They ask that we be loving, calm, caring, attentive, trusting, playful, honest, and mature. All the things that a thoughtful person is striving to be. It has been said that adults do not create children but rather that children create adults.

That is not to say that there will not be times in everyone's work-life that our jobs will demand long hours and exhausting schedules. As long as this is the exception and not the rule, there is little danger here. If, however, we are working within an environment that demands a commitment in time and energy which throws other important areas of our lives into disarray on an ongoing basis, we should consider whether we have created a situation that is truly in our own best interests. If we believe we have not, and if it cannot be corrected within our present circumstances, we may need to leave and seek a business, career, company, or boss that requires less of our time and energy and still feels that we are committed and doing a good job.

At different times of our lives we are able to devote more time to our jobs and still remain balanced. When we are single and have few family commitments, we can work long hours and still have time to handle other important areas of our lives, i.e., our bodies, our homes, our friends, ourselves. When we are married, our relationship with our spouse will require quality time and this must be fitted in without throwing the other areas off. Children must be given both quality *and* quantity time, especially in their early years. As they enter their teen years their need for our time diminishes, though perhaps to a lesser degree than we often realize. When they leave home, the time they need from us greatly diminishes and the time we have available for other areas of our lives increases.

Our lives run in cycles and we need to learn to be aware of what is asked of us in each of our different cycles. There is a season for all things. We need to continually ask ourselves what season of our lives we are in. If we have very young children it may not be the best time to start a new business or make a career change or take on a project that will require the majority of our attention and time. If we are single or without children or if our child-rearing days are ending or diminishing, it may be just the time. Beware though, that if our business life demands so much of us that there is just not enough time and energy left to be fair to our family, we may need to adjust our business commitments. Few on their deathbed ever said "I wish I had spent more time at the office."

If we can return to a model that assumes a totally benevolent Universe and one in which guidance will be clear as we let go of our fears, we can assume that in being guided towards our Highest Good we will always be able to have the time and energy needed to handle, in a balanced fashion, our most sacred relationships, those of our family and friends. The job, career, or business that is right for us will allow this. By remembering this, we can begin to teach our children an unwavering trust in the goodness of the world, in spite of its trials and tribulations.

Following this concept often takes trust and courage. If our present situation is not allowing this balance we must trust that when we set about to change it, the end result will support our purpose in being on the planet, i.e., to teach an learn love. Once we are busy working on this assigned task, our mission, peace of mind and balance, must follow. Peace of mind, because we will finally feel that what we are doing fits and is right for us. Balance because balance is an essential ingredient inherent in our mission. No one is sent here to be off-balance. Our work cannot be correctly accomplished from that state. Until we are working on our mission, we will always feel restless and searching. We are not doing what we were sent to do. We are not being who we really are.

We may not be able to perceive this end result when we begin the process of change. Any movement towards a more balanced life is a movement towards this goal, whether we are aware of it or not. Sometimes the changes are as simple as making the inner decision to devote more of our time and energy to our families and then making needed adjustments in our schedules. Even this takes a certain level of trust and a quieting of the fears that tell us less work equals less productivity, less money, fewer accomplishments, or fewer promotions. We can address these fears by continually reminding ourselves that we are meant to lead a balanced life. The work that we are meant to do, the accomplishments that we are meant to accomplish, the money that we are meant to have, will be provided form this place of balance.

Few on their deathbed ever said "I wish I had spent more time at the office."

Other times, greater changes in our outer life may be needed. The nature of our existing circumstances may make a balanced life impossible. We may need to confront our employers, partners, or clients with the dilemma and ask for their support in our goal to balance our life. We may be surprised to find it is an issue for them too. If however, we find that they are unwilling to support this goal because they feel it is of little value compared to the work they want us to accomplish (in those long hours and all-encompassing commitment), then greater trust and courage may be needed. It may require the termination of these relationships. This usually means changing jobs, careers, partners, or businesses.

However, just our willingness to share with others our desire for a more balanced life will be a lesson, for both us and them, in love. This may be hard for us to recognize, especially if their response is ridicule, anger, indifference, or disagreement. Still, it will serve as a reminder to them, though perhaps initially unheeded, that relationships are of the highest importance and that the work that is meant for us will allow time and energy for our key relationships. It is not our responsibility that those around us remember this, or even agree that there is something to remember. It is only our responsibility to *ourselves* to remember and awaken. And our remembering and awakening is also the greatest service we can offer them.

Little or no change would be possible if a complete absence of fear were first required.

It is very difficult to put our entire career, income, and/or business on the line in the effort to bring our lives into balance. An understanding is needed that a balanced life is both our goal and our birthright, as it is for every being on the planet. Every other animal species lives in balance in their day-to-day life (except animals domesticated and influenced by man). Fish are not stressed out, birds do not ignore their young, nor are squirrels too rushed. Why should humans, the most advanced of all species, not deserve the same?

This is not to say that fear will not surface while contemplating change. It will. We just need to continue to release the fear so that it does not control us. We do not need an absolute trust or a total absence of fear. Little or no change would be possible if a complete absence of fear were first required. Our fear will be brought under control if we have an understanding, and eventually the faith, that there exist specific missions in all areas of our lives (especially our work and family lives) and that these missions can only be effectively accomplished if we are well balanced in all key aspects of our lives. If this faith has not yet been established within us, just a willingness to find a better way will put the process in motion.

It may feel like jumping off a cliff into the unknown, to trust that we will be provided for, to trust that our desire to lead a balanced life will set things in motion and bring this to us in ways we could never have imagined. If we do not have this belief, or if it is only starting to develop, we may find it almost impossible to trust to the point where we put our income, career, and financial stability on the line. If greater fear is created by leaving our present circumstances at this time, then this should be avoided until these fears are reduced to a manageable level. Moving towards balance will never involve a heightening of fear.

Until these fears are below the threshold of dominating our thoughts and behavior, continuing in the present situation may be the best course. Our lessons are not yet complete in these circumstances and when they are, the circumstances will change. Our willingness to find a better way will keep the process flowing. Each of us is learning at our own self-imposed pace and we can sense when we are truly ready to confront each fear. To do so before we are ready will only heighten it.

Usually great leaps of faith are not needed. The desire to balance our life and our willingness to make the required changes will often open the way for these changes to be brought to us and often in gentle ways. Usually these are slowly-evolving changes in which time is allowed to correct any misperceptions or mistakes in our existing situation. Healing any conflict or lack of forgiveness in existing relationships and / or resolving certain fears are often required for our next, more balanced step to become clear to us. Otherwise, the old thought-system could create a similar situation but in a new setting. We may be trying to impose a geographical or logistical solution onto an emotional or spiritual problem. We may be trying to alter the outer without creating true inner change.

To avoid re-creating similar imbalance and pain in a new setting, it is important that we understand the source of the conflict or pain in our existing circumstance. If we are blaming the "problem" on things external to us (the job requirements, the boss, the client, the economy, the industry), then we have misperceived the situation and have understood neither the source of the pain nor its function. It is likely that a similarly painful situation will be created over and over until the source is perceived. The source of our pain, no matter how often we would like to place it elsewhere, is always within ourselves. The function of all pain is to show us when we are still fearful. The presence of any fear is a sure sign that we are trusting in our strength alone. If we begin to trust in the strength of a benevolent Universe and a loving God, our fears will subside.

Pain serves as a motivator, as every being strives to reduce or remove pain, no matter how misguided or clumsy the attempt. If the source of the pain is correctly understood, the attempt to reduce it will be successful. As we examine the sources of our pain we will find that they are often fear-based illusions. If the source is misperceived and misunderstood, the attempt to alleviate it must fail since we cannot correctly solve a problem that has been incorrectly diagnosed.

It is easy to think that the source of our pain is outside ourselves. However, pain is an internal emotion and therefore always responsive to our efforts. Pain is an internal response to an external stimulus. If we are fired or lose our job (an external stimulus), we feel pain (an internal response). Why? Usually because the external stimulus has also triggered our internal fears. We fear that we will not find a better job, that the situation points to an internal flaw in us, that there will not be enough money, that we are slipping down the mountain we are trying to climb, or that we will lose the respect of others.

If we viewed the Universe as benevolent and loving and offering us only gifts in the form of lessons to be learned, we would view a job loss as a new chapter beginning. We would trust that everything we needed would be provided and that the new chapter could offer us even more than the old. Pain, though common, is not necessary in this situation. The choice is ours. A vivid example of this attitude was recently demonstrated by a famous pitcher. At the height of his career, cancer was discovered in his pitching arm. He underwent treatment and was determined to return to pitching, the job he loved and had worked on and perfected throughout his life. The treatment seemed successful and he returned to the mound the next year. Shortly after his return something remarkable happened. It was remarkable because, to most people, who believe in a random or punitive Universe, it would have been a tragedy. To him it was a miracle and a blessing. During one of the season games, he threw a pitch and his arm broke. He knew that if that ever happened the treatment had not been effective and that it would not only mean the end of his career but also the loss of his arm and shoulder.

When we are tired enough or when the pain is intense enough, we will seek change.

In his first press conference after the operation to remove his arm and shoulder, this man made a remarkable statement. He said that at the moment that his arm broke he had two incredible emotions. The first was intense physical pain. The other was incredible joy in the realization that God had other plans for him besides pitching. He said that the loss of his career and arm had caused him some depression but not crippling despair; he understood that everything, no matter how painful or tragic it might seem, is a gift and a lesson. There was nothing to fear about the future because his path would always be clear and rewarding. He had no idea what his next chapter, his next mission would be, but he knew that as long as he was open to guidance he would be directed onto the right path. He also understood that his fight with cancer and the loss of his arm were essential lessons to prepare him for this next mission.

This episode was also a miracle in that it affected millions of people, though they may not have understood it on a conscious level. His dilemma was observed and known to millions of fans. As with all great baseball players, he was the idol of many children. They all felt his pain and loss. However, to the millions of people who heard or read his response at the press conference, he taught us a lesson of love. We all had an opportunity to learn, especially the children, that other, more uplifting responses are available to us, even in what appear to be the most tragic of circumstances. He taught that we need not be attached to any one career or job or accomplishment, but only to remember that everything in life is a blessing and that fulfillment and peace are always available to us. We need only open to the next chapter, as one chapter ends. It does not matter whether we have chosen to end the chapter, or whether another person or circumstance ends it for us.

If we examine our innermost thoughts and feelings (especially our most dominant ones), we will find that certain fears have caused many of our painful situations. If we uncover and examine these fears we can come to understand that they are groundless. In a truly benign Universe, pain is an indication of a mistake or misperception that needs correction and "tragedy" is often a turning point towards greater freedom. Fear is not appropriate, for there is nothing to fear.

Our choice, then, is to begin this search for a more balanced work situation or to continue to remain in the situation that is causing important areas of our life to remain out-of-balance. These unbalanced situations will continue to be painful as our close relationships and inner peace continue to deteriorate, even as our successes in our careers may continue to grow. This pain will be a constant signal to us of where a correction is needed.

Being is important, not doing and owning.

It is likely that eventually the pain will grow too intense or the struggle too tiring. This pain or weariness is a blessing in the same way that the pain of placing our hand on a hot stovetop makes us remove it or weariness makes us sleep. When we are tired enough or when the pain is intense enough, we will seek change. In the beginning we may simply seek change to end the pain or get some rest. This is often our initial motivation. But something very special happens when we begin to attempt to ease this pain or find rest. We have put into motion subtle yet powerful forces, triggered by the one thought, weak as it may be in the beginning, that says, "I am tired of being out-of-balance. There must be a better way. What is it?" Though we may not understand this at the beginning, we are beginning to make the decision that we no longer want to be controlled by the fears that caused us to create the situation in the first place. We are starting to question this inner fear-based programming. If we search long enough and ask enough questions, we will see that our fears are groundless, they are born of a mistaken sense of lack of self-worth. We will recognize that we were programmed to believe that our value lies in what we do, not who we are. In truth, being is important, not doing and owning.

In the course of contemplating these changes, fear may seem not only appropriate, but required. Viewed from another frame of reference, this need not be so. As we move towards a balanced life, we are moving towards where we are meant to be, i.e., a place of balance. Whatever is meant to happen from this place, is for our Highest Good. We will rediscover that the Universe is a totally benign place and that we are deserving of, and rightfully due, balance and peace in our work and family life.

> **L**isted below are commonly
> accepted principles and their underlying
> fears. Score yourself on a scale from 1 to
> 10 to see how your present thoughts
> and emotions are formed by these
> principles and fears.

Accepted Principles

1 My worklife is of greater importance than my family life.   _____

2 By continually working long hours, I am serving my family by providing the financial stability they need.   _____

3 Our family members will understand if we break commitments or cannot be there for them. Our bosses, clients, or customers will not. _____

4 Time spent with the family and in relationships is not as valuable as time spent accomplishing tasks in our work. _____

5 If a business endeavor is financially "successful," then it is successful. _____

6 To be successful in our business life, we must be willing to place our families second to our work. _____

7 To be successful, we must be willing to work fifty, sixty, seventy, or more hours each week. _____

8 A lack of interest or attention that results in emotional pain to our loved ones is more acceptable to us than one that results in our achieving less in our worklife. _____

9 Family commitments can be broken but work commitments must be kept. Family members are more forgiving. _____

10 If we are not willing to place our work above our family, we may lose our promotion, client, raise, or business to someone who is. _____

11 It is reasonable and fair for our business and/or employer to demand that we put our work ahead of our family and ask for long hours and/or separations from the family. _____

12 Many opportunities in business may not come again. Opportunities with the family usually come again. _____

13 Children need very little from their parents until they are the age when they can reason and communicate clearly to us. _____

14 A simple family event (picnic, movie, night at home, children's rehearsal, etc.) is not as important or productive as a business commitment. _____

Fears Underlying
Accepted Principles

1 I fear that I am not of value if I do not produce tangible results. I am of value for what I do, not for who I am. _____

2 In business I deal with logic. In relationships I must deal with emotions. This is frightening to me because many of my emotions are not logical. _____

3 I am afraid there will be a lack of money to supply my needs. _____

4 I fear that if I do not give my work almost all of my attention, I will fail or not reach my greatest success. _____

5 I need to stay busy doing something. If I slow down I may not feel good about myself. Business accomplishments validate my self-worth. _____

6 I fear that if I am not willing to give almost everything to my work I will not be perceived as truly committed. _____

7 My family relationships are already somewhat of a failure and I fear that I am unable to bring them into a loving balance. _____

8 If I give the needed time to my children I will not have enough time for my work. _____

9 In my worklife, the rules are clear and I understand how to succeed at the game. In intimate relationships, the rules are never clear and I am not as confident I will succeed. _____

"Tragedy" is often a turning point
towards greater freedom.

Our goal is peace of mind. Our purpose is to teach and learn love. Every decision can be evaluated according to how successfully it accomplishes this purpose and leads to this goal. Everything that is meant for us and that is for our Highest Good, every job, every promotion, every sum of money will be the result of our clear and ethical behavior and never of our fearful behavior. As we are guided towards balanced growth and development, we will never be asked to compromise our ethics, our integrity, or our complete honesty. If a situation or a person is asking for this compromise from us, it is an opportunity to reexamine our relationship and resolve any fears we may have. If an ethical compromise is still required from us, it is a sign that we need to change or leave that relationship.

Ethics: Everyday Opportunities

Ethics and our personal codes of business conduct is the everyday arena wherein we have a chance to choose, on a day-by-day, moment to moment basis, love and peace or fear and pain. This arena will just as often involve minor everyday situations as it will major life choices. Anytime we do or say anything that makes us uncomfortable from an ethical standpoint, we are choosing fear. When our ethical decisions create peace within us, we are choosing love and trust. If our goal is peace, it is clear which we must choose.

Because our species is still young and fear is still the dominant emotion (though this is quickly changing now as we awaken), our actions often do not follow our inner sense of what is honest, fair, and just. In the early stages of our development, when we are totally oblivious to who we are and why we are here, ethical and moral questions are not, as yet, even issues for us. For most of us however, these are issues. All too often we have built an entire framework of intelligent rationalizations in our attempt to justify the actions that contradict our deepest sense of right and wrong. The problem with this system of rationalization is that it really does not work. Though this system of rationalization *is* successful at temporarily placating our fears, it does not succeed in helping us understand or release them. It placates fears by allowing behavior that will lead to outcomes that our fearful emotions have convinced us are essential for our survival. However, at a deep and powerful level, this fearful behavior continues to drain our peace of mind and self-esteem. It does this in two ways.

First, by our continuing this pattern, we are reinforcing the fear-based programming and subsequent fearful behavior. We are being run by our fears, seeking to placate them, instead of confronting and resolving them. Second, since the fear-based behavior contradicts our truest and deepest vision and desire as to how to treat others and operate in this world, the conflict continually and constantly drains our self-esteem and peace of mind.

The resolution to this dilemma is to begin to trust and understand that in creating outcomes in any situation that will be for the benefit of all involved, these outcomes will never require compromises in our basic code of integrity, justice, and ethics. This will be the shortest path to our goal, happiness and peace of mind.

Situations in both our personal and worklives that involve ethical and moral issues are some of the most important we will encounter. It is in these situations, and the decisions we make regarding them, that we are given the opportunity to choose once again fear or love. It is here where much of our growth as individuals occurs. It is also in these areas that we directly teach and learn either love or fear.

Many of these situations seem small and insignificant. They will often appear as simply the normal way of doing business in the world. We cheat on our taxes or expense account. We tell a small "white lie" in our business dealings. We say nothing when we are given too much change. We omit information we know someone should know but that might jeopardize our chances to get what we want. We do not honor the agreements we have made with others. These things often seem to be inconsequential and of little or no significance, but they represent a set of fear-based principles and their subsequent pattern of behavior that has a great effect on the way we perceive and feel about ourselves.

These situations and our fearful decisions regarding them, may appear so mundane and common as to disappear into the background of our lives. They have become "normal" ways of doing business. The fact that they have become so "normal" and so accepted, is part of the reason why the "normal" person is experiencing limited happiness or peace. We are often doing many small acts each day that, at a deep level, do not feel right to us but have become an accepted part of our everyday behavior.

For each of these acts we have a rationalization so that on a mental level we have justified them. However, our emotions are always more powerful than our thoughts. On an emotional level, they may remain unjustified and unresolved and thereby sap our inner peace and sense of self-worth. They contribute to confusion, guilt, and pain as they rob our self-esteem. They contribute to dysfunctional families, divorce, and loneliness as they undermine our relationships. They contribute to ulcers, cancer, and heart attacks, as our inner fears and conflicts attack our bodies.

Our emotions are always more powerful than our thoughts.

When confronted with a fearful situation, it is best to step back from the fears and emotions involved and to acknowledge and understand that this is an important and crucial situation involving our growth and the growth of all those involved. Then identify and name the major fears that the situation is triggering in us (and if possible identify them in the other people involved). Having identified these fears we need to confront and resolve them realizing that in a totally benevolent Universe, fears are never appropriate.

Often identifying the fears is the easiest part and confronting them the most difficult. Again, it will take an adjustment in how we have come to view the Universe that will dictate how we respond. If we consider our Universe to be random or punitive, fears are appropriate and need to be respected and given the power to influence and control our behavior. In a random Universe it is appropriate to fear "bad luck" and in a punitive Universe, punishment. In a benevolent Universe, fears are never appropriate and need to be recognized, understood, and released so as to have a minimal effect on our behavior and never become the deciding factor.

If we peel the layers of our fears back far enough, we will often discover that their main source is the fear that we are not worthy, that we are unlovable. We fear we are not worthy of financial stability and abundance, of job fulfillment, of respectful treatment, of a balanced worklife. We fear we are unworthy because we have temporarily forgotten who we are. We mistakenly believe we are only physical bodies, inhabited by egos, with all their flaws and fears. We have forgotten that we are all children of a benevolent and loving Creator, deserving of all His gifts. It is only our forgetting that leads to this fearful behavior. It is our remembering that will correct this behavior.

In addition to the many daily ethical dilemmas, we will be given, as blessings, several major ethical/moral decisions in any given period of our lives. These major situations will correspond to and be created by our major fears. These major issues are also our greatest blessings in that they provide us the opportunity to confront, understand, and resolve our dominant fears, fears that may be influencing many areas of our lives. We will recognize these major life situations by how large the stakes seem. The greater the fear the more intense the situation will appear, with major ramifications for many involved. It may involve large sums of money, someone's job, promotion, reputation, or feelings. An employer may ask us to lie or steal. A large sum of money may ride on our telling the truth. We may have made a mistake that has caused pain, harm, or loss to another and need to take responsibility for it and make amends. However, it may also appear as an insignificant situation that has caused someone great harm or pain. We need to understand that the people and the situations are not there "by accident." Each has a definite role to play. All have the same lesson to learn, to release their fears and judgments and allow love and trust to emerge into the situation, in order to allow the miracle to occur.

We also need to understand that these fears have been part of us for a long time, perhaps for most of our lives. Situations will trigger these fears at various times. These situations are always blessings or opportunities for us to release our fears though they are often perceived as curses, punishments, or bad luck. Usually we will precipitate a major incident that triggers the fear to its greatest intensity just when we are finally ready to understand and let go of it. This may appear very frightening to us. If we fear rejection or lack of money, our job or financial security may become threatened. If we fear confrontation or encountering someone else's judgment, rejection, disapproval, or anger, we may create a circumstance where our principles or perception runs contrary to someone else's and where one only may prevail in the situation, with major ramifications for the parties involved. If we fear we are not good enough or have not accomplished enough, we may confront a possible major "failure."

The thought of reacting entirely differently from our usual fear-based response may appear so frightening that it is almost unimaginable to us. Could we really confront our boss or client? Could we really tell the truth or say what we think, even if it meant that the outcome was not the most desirable financially? Could we really live true to our code of ethics even if it meant being fired or not advancing as quickly? Could we really trust that we would be peacefully guided towards our next job or opportunity instead of remaining in a compromising situation or fearfully grasping at whatever becomes available to us? Remember that in these circumstances, fear and the ego are making a tremendous effort to convince us they are valid and should be listened to and obeyed. Whatever the fears, until they are confronted and released, they will cause us to continually create painful situations. The pain is our alarm that a fear is present that needs to be resolved so the alarm can be turned off. The alarm will stay on till it is no longer needed.

Often we interpret these situations as proof that the fears are indeed valid. We get fired or incur disapproval of an employer, proving that we are unworthy, incompetent, and/or unlovable. We fail at an endeavor proving that we are not good enough. We confront someone and incur their anger, rejection, and/or judgment proving that they must be right and we must be wrong or at fault for their pain. It is easy to understand how these outcomes seem to prove that the fears are all valid. Viewed from another perspective, the outcomes of the situations are created by our fears. They are not proof that the fears are valid, only that they are still present.

If the fears had been overcome, a different outcome would have been possible or the situation avoided entirely. People with high self-esteem and no fears regarding their self-worth, make excellent employees and are seldom fired, and if so, seldom for good cause. Without fears, "failures" are fewer and when encountered viewed as learning experiences, not failures. After fears are released, confrontations are reduced and another person's anger, rejection, and/or disapproval is acceptable as we realize we cannot, and should not try, to please anyone by compromising our values.

To add to this confusion, we often observe actions that exhibit little or no integrity and yet result in career or financial "rewards," sometimes very great rewards. Many of the people who have become the most "successful" financially or in their careers, seem to be the ones demonstrating little or no integrity or honesty. Their "success" would seem to indicate that not only is their behavior acceptable, but even desirable. If this behavior is *not* creating their Highest Good, why do they seem to be rewarded instead of punished?

Possessions and achievements will never, of themselves, offer us happiness.

The fact is, they are being neither punished nor rewarded. They are simply "reaping what they sow." If fear and/or desire for material gain or accomplishment are the dominant emotions, then pain will be their greatest reward, no matter how it may appear on the outside. Possessions and achievements will never, of themselves, offer us happiness. The results appear as rewards and as successes only because we have forgotten our goal and purpose.

Because we have created and reinforced the illusion that we are primarily physical, not spiritual, beings, we have convinced ourselves that things on the physical plane, i.e., success, accomplishments, cars, money, houses, etc. will bring us peace of mind and happiness. We view these as indicators of our success as human beings and therefore need to be better than as many as possible in order to find self-esteem. In doing this we have made success in their eyes more important than feeling at peace with our own decisions.

If we feel our purpose is to amass the greatest amount of wealth or to keep or progress in our jobs, then to the degree our decisions support these purposes, these goals are achieved. Hence, people whose goal is accumulation of money or accomplishment are usually successful at attaining this goal. Our world will always reflect back to us our deepest desires and fears (emotions). The illusion here, is that achieving these goals will also bring peace and happiness. But history is full of examples of wealthy and / or accomplished individuals who found little peace of mind or happiness.

In a certain way "successes" attained through compromise of one's integrity are their own punishment, not punishment meted out by a punitive God but rather the natural painful results of fear-based behavior. To have been rewarded with financial or career success at the cost of true peace of mind and high self-esteem found by following our highest principles, is to have sacrificed something of real and lasting value for trinkets. The quantity of trinkets we have amassed does not matter. We have traded trinkets for gold.

Initially, and for a limited period, possessing the trinkets may be exhilarating and pleasant. Since success is still being measured in faulty terms, the world may agree that we are indeed successful. If the trinkets were attained with the illusion that they might offer us peace of mind or happiness, we will experience only disappointment, not particularly pain. But we all know the feeling of finally getting something we very much desired only to soon realize it has not really changed the way we feel or our level of enjoyment in life, as we thought it might. If, however, these accomplishments or possessions were attained by the sacrifice of our integrity and honesty, the subsequent loss of self-esteem and peace will cause pain. This is why so many people are constantly involved in business ("busyness"). By keeping busy and distracted, we can avoid this pain temporarily, but eventually it will resurface. The pain will once again be a blessing to alert us to an area of our life that we need to change by allowing love and trust, not fear, to rule. The pain will continue until the change has been made and the alert signal is no longer needed.

We may feel that it is not really fear that is causing us to act against our best ethical instincts, but rather our desires. We desire the promotion, the job, the money, the possessions so much that fearful and unethical behavior is acceptable. Our minds are usually able to provide rationalizations for any behavior that allows us to obtain anything we deeply desire. The physical plane is indeed an alluring realm. With its pleasures and sensations, it is easy to understand how we come under its spell. However, we must be wary, for desires that are powerful enough to cause us to act against our own best principles often have fear as their basis. We must remember that our purpose should always be centered around our relationships, with ourselves and others, not around our possessions or our accomplishments, which are just tools.

This is not to say that our possessions and accomplishments are inherently valueless (or inherently valuable) and should not be enjoyed. Their value is established by the consciousness of the person interacting with them. Correctly perceived, they are blessings, the result of our love and clarity of purpose. Our efforts, based on this clarity, will produce all the achievements and possessions that are meant for us and for our Highest Good. They are not the source of our peace and self-esteem, but rather their tangible outgrowth. They will always be exactly what we need, no more and no less.

If we begin to accept that we have a purpose on earth, our views begin to change and our course of action realigns itself with this purpose. If we believe that we are here to learn and teach love and to remove all blocks and fears to our love, then each decision can be evaluated by how closely it serves this purpose. We can ask ourselves, "What is the most loving course of action? What will assist in removing the illusions that I am presently living under?" And, "Will this action teach love or fear?" To the degree our decisions support this purpose determines whether it will bring us happiness and peace. If we believe, even if only for a moment, that the Universe is always guiding us to act ethically and in ways that do not create internal conflict or to avoid or change situations that are guiding us otherwise, then we will begin to make decisions differently. In every situation, the question of our purpose and which decisions best support our purpose emerge.

Once we have correctly perceived our true purpose, the fears will, for a period of time, remain as an obstacle to accomplishing this purpose. They have been with us a long time and our egos have convinced us they are necessary for our survival. One effective method of getting past these deeply ingrained fears is to begin to understand the joy and freedom that will be available to us once we have conquered them, instead of having allowed them to conquer us. It is as if for our entire lives we have gone over and over along the same path until we arrived at a large, high wall (our fears) that would allow us to go no further. We have always stopped at the wall and do not even know what is on the other side. The wall appears so high and impenetrable that anything other than stopping there (acting out of fear) seems unimaginable. However, once we have decided that there must be a better way, the change begins (*Course*, text, p. 18). When we have begun to understand our fears, we have scaled to the top of the wall. Once we have conquered and resolved our fears, they no longer dictate our behavior. The wall is behind us and no longer impedes our progress and growth. We have never been on the other side of the wall. On the other side there are new adventures, new sights, and new feelings. On the other side we are free of our fears and the painful circumstances they created. On the other side is greater peace and happiness.

If we begin to accept that we have a purpose on earth, our views begin to change.

The wall may appear in many forms in our worklife. Our wall may be the fear that we will not have financial security or career success if we leave a job or field we have invested years of work in and pursue a different one that may offer greater fulfillment. The well-worn path is our everyday decision to continue at our present job. The other side of this wall is our life with more fulfilling work. Or maybe our wall is our fear of confronting someone in our worklife who has been treating us unfairly or demanding fear-based actions from us. Our well-worn path is our allowing this to continually occur. Scaling this wall is realizing our worth, realizing that we were not sent to be treated or to respond in this way and then nonjudgmentally confronting the other person. The other side of this wall is our life without this painful treatment and / or relationship.

The wall may be our fear to operate totally honestly and ethically in our workplace. The well-worn path is our less than honest day-to-day behavior. We can scale this wall by remembering that we were sent with a purpose that includes and requires total honesty and integrity. The other side of the wall is the freedom of a life that involves no sacrifice in our code of ethics.

By keeping clear in our mind the invalid and faulty basis of our fears as well as the uplifting benefits we will gain by finally conquering our fears, we can actually reach a state where we are eagerly anticipating, instead of dreading, the circumstances that will allow us to confront this fear. Recognizing this fear and acknowledging that the power we have given it was inappropriate and out of proportion will begin the process. We can look forward to conquering and being free of the fear and experiencing the peace and clarity this freedom offers. Just knowing that we are finally confronting this ancient fear can bring us joy. It may be a statement we need to make to someone or an action we need to initiate that is different from the fear-based ones of our past. When the time comes to finally confront a situation and take the action or make the statement that is based on our highest principles instead of our fear, we may feel anxious and nervous, as we are confronting a major change in our life. We are scaling the wall. However, mixed in with this anxiety will be a sense of excitement we may remember as children when it was our first day of school or camp or as a teenager when we left home or went to college. It was both scary and exciting. It was new and challenging. But above all it was something that we knew we had to do and very much wanted to do.

Once the fear is confronted and conquered, it may reappear but it will have a greatly diminished hold on us and will no longer dictate our behavior. It may be one of many emotions we feel but it will no longer be the dominant one. It may continue to cause us some anxiety and worry but we will be able to reestablish our peace and clarity as we once again evaluate our fears and place them within our new perspective. A major change will have taken place in this area of our life as trust, love, and self-esteem replace fear and self-condemnation as our dominant emotions. Fulfillment, peace, and joy will replace conflict, pain, and confusion. We will find that the sun shines more brightly on the other side of the wall.

Following this course towards our Higher Purpose sometimes results in apparent success and advantages on the physical and financial plane. But this is not always the case. It may be as we follow our own inner guidance the decision we make may lead away from what appears to be our best interests in the area of finances or careers. At first it may appear that we must sacrifice in order to apply these principles. This is not really so. We are always guided to our Highest Good. If we have lost some financial reward but instead increased our self-respect and peace of mind, doesn't this make us happier? In essence, we have avoided spending energy on an illusion of happiness—the possessions or accomplishments—and have gone directly to its true source—peace of mind. We have only sacrificed the time, pain, and energy spent trying to grasp an illusion.

We will no longer use financial and career criteria as the dominant determinant in our decision making. We will trust that if a deal does not happen or a job is lost, a better one will appear as we follow our course, a better one because it possesses integrity and balance. This path may at first appear "painful." It may appear as a net loss; someone may be angry with us, we may lose money, a job, or a client. However, this perception of loss or sacrifice is an illusion. We will never need to sacrifice anything that will bring us peace. If we have successfully conquered the fear that causes us to act against our own ethics and integrity, these situations, and the results of our decisions regarding them, are as they should be. They no longer need to cause us any pain. The pain is no longer needed to alert us that we are out-of-balance and have forgotten our purpose.

For others involved in the situation, pain may or may not be needed in this and similar situations to serve as an alert to them. We do not need to blame ourselves for their pain nor judge them for still needing it. Everyone has their own learning process and pace of learning. This process, no matter how it may appear on the surface, is always a blessing.

If we find ourselves resistant to determining our course of action from a sense of honesty and integrity and resistant to viewing business situations in these terms, we need to remind ourselves that we will be guided towards our greatest growth and development by following these principles. If we must act against our inner sense of integrity to keep or advance in our job, or for our company or idea to succeed, then the job, the money, the promotion, or the success is not meant for us. We must trust that a compromise of our highest values would not be required if it were meant for us.

This approach makes decision making much easier. The tangible results of our decisions are no longer the basis for the decision but only one facet to be considered. It is the decision itself, and the impact it will have on others, that is important. Was it made according to our highest principles? Does it compromise our honesty and integrity? Will it lead to greater peace of mind and self-esteem? Will it teach love or fear? Our true path can always be discerned as we begin to perceive the peace created by our clear and courageous decisions and actions.

By acting from our highest principles, we can trust and find peace in knowing that the subsequent results are meant for us and will result in the highest good for all involved. We discover we have taught and learned love. A miracle has entered the situation. We have been successful at what we were sent here to do. This is the only true success.

> **L**isted below are commonly accepted principles and their underlying fears. Score yourself on a scale from 1 to 10 to see how your present thoughts and emotions are formed by these principles and fears.

Accepted Principles

1 Sometimes, to achieve the greatest success, it is necessary to look the other way in areas of business ethics. _____

2 Everyone does it. It is the way things are done in this business. Why should I be any different? _____

3 If I want to keep my job (or advance in my career or make the most money), I must sometimes do things that I am uncomfortable with on an ethical level. _____

4 No individual is being victimized in this situation. No one person is hurt by these actions. Why not do it? _____

5 This area is not black or white. It is a shade of grey, and though I am not completely comfortable with this course of action, everything is relative and who's to say what is right or wrong? _____

6 If I do not do it, someone else will. Why shouldn't it be me?   _____

7 The ethics of business are different from those used in my personal life.   _____

8 If I do not follow the existing and accepted code of ethics and behavior, I will be fired (lose money, not advance, etc.).   _____

9 If it is not illegal, then it is an acceptable course of behavior.   _____

10 If someone is not clever enough to protect themselves from my deception, they deserve the results.   _____

11 If the end is "successful" financially, it is proof that the means are justified.   _____

12 I am due more by this company (person, client, boss) than I get. Therefore, less than honest behavior to get what I deserve is justified.   _____

Fears Underlying
Accepted Principles

1 I fear I will fail, or not obtain my maximum success, if I am not willing to do things that sometimes do not agree with my sense of ethics.   _____

2 Everyone is doing it. I fear if I respond differently I will not be liked, accepted, or asked to be involved. I may appear as a threat to their accepted system of thought.   _____

3 I fear the Universe is operating on lack and limited supply and I must get what I need, no matter what that means.   _____

4 I have fears regarding relationships with people. Possessions and accomplishments can fill this void and give me what I need.   _____

5 I fear without money, success, and achievements, I will not be happy or at peace.   _____

6 I fear I cannot be successful by always following a course of action that is compatible with my sense of business integrity.   _____

The Universe is a place of abundance but it also responds to certain laws. One of these laws is that the outer manifestation of the different areas of our lives will always reflect our innermost and dominant thoughts and emotions regarding each area of our lives. These inner thoughts and emotions are then directed through our will to create our outer lives. We therefore control our financial condition by creating it through our will, which is fueled by our thoughts and emotions.

If we resolve our fears regarding our lack of money, at least to a point that they no longer dominate and control us, we will always be provided with all the money we need to sustain ourselves and our families and to accomplish our goals and missions. Which rung of the financial ladder we are on is of little consequence. Our work and lives will begin to be guided by our trust and awareness of purpose, rather than by our fear of not having enough money.

CHAPTER 4

Money: Where Does It Come From?

It is a common and easily accepted concept that many national recessions are caused or deepened and extended, not by the financial realities of the country's economy, but rather by the people's confidence level in, and perceptions of, their nation's economy at the time. That, simply, the thoughts and emotions of citizens create the national financial climate, rather than the climate creating their thoughts and emotions. Of course, once the climate is set, it tends to solidify and justify these thoughts and emotions. Here, the human thoughts and emotions are the cause of the financial conditions, not the effect.

Though this is easy for us to understand and accept on a national level, it is much harder to accept on a personal level. What we view in the macrocosms of our nations, we are slow to perceive and accept in the microcosms of our personal lives. However, it is as true for us personally as it is for us nationally. The financial condition of our personal lives is a direct outer reflection of our thoughts and emotions regarding prosperity and poverty, abundance and lack. Our thoughts and emotions regarding our prosperity are directed by our will and, in turn, create our financial condition. We are self-generating and self-directed magnets, drawing to ourselves whatever we choose.

If we are satisfied or pleased with our financial condition, we have no problem taking full credit at having created this condition ourselves. Deep down though, we may feel that this prosperous condition is really not under our control and not of our making and that it could deteriorate at any time and we would be unable to restore it. We may claim to have created our financial stability or prosperity, but in reality, we may fear we do not control it.

On the other hand, if we are not satisfied with our financial situation, it is much easier to blame it on conditions outside of ourselves, over which we have no control. We can blame it on the recession, the career or business we are in, the boss or company we work for, the family expenses we have, a poor decision we made, or lack of education or training. It is always simpler to blame conditions outside ourselves, than to search within for negative attitudes and fears that may be creating the outer conditions we lament. It is simpler but not easier, because we are prolonging these painful conditions caused by our fears, rather than confronting and resolving them. Only the resolution of these fears will place our financial destinies back under the conscious control of our clarity and trust. We are where we are financially because of who we are.

At first it may be fearful to accept the premise that our thoughts and emotions are creating our financial condition, as we tend to perceive ourselves as unable to control the long ingrained patterns that are the source of our thoughts and emotions. It seems easier to try to change the conditions in our outer lives than to try to change ourselves. When we encounter painful or fearful situations we usually scramble to ease the pain or placate our fears rather than quietly turn within to seek and understand the source of the negative programming that has caused the particular condition.

The concept that resolving and changing lifetime patterns of thinking and feeling is extremely difficult, if not impossible, is supported by what we have observed in the world around us. People seem to run on automatic pilot their whole lifetime, their behavior controlled by inner programs set in place twenty, thirty, or forty years earlier.

Dramatic change often seems to occur only when a major event shatters our world and forces us to begin an inner search in order to relieve the pain. A death, divorce, loss of health, financial disaster, or other difficult event may trigger this search. When it occurs, accompanied by intense pain, it is frequently perceived as a personal catastrophe, with no positive implications. As the pain eases, if properly interpreted, this event may be understood as one of our greatest gifts.

We are where we are financially because of who we are.

Professional psychotherapists often seem to have limited success helping their patients in freeing themselves from lifelong patterns, only helping after many years of analysis or the use of drugs. Since it is often their ego that is attempting to alter their patient's ego, the process may be described as "an illusion treating an illusion for an illusion." This is not to say that there is no value to professional help. Just by the process of devoting their lives to the task of psychotherapeutically assisting others, professionals can offer some level of healing to their patients. However, if the therapist and patient both still perceive our Universe as random or punitive, they will reinforce and solidify this illusion in each other. In doing so, they may teach the ego to more effectively function but only within their limited view of the world, and thus, true healing will not yet have occurred. We can only teach what we learn. The most effective psychotherapists, whether professional or "lay" therapists, are those who have resolved their own fears or are willing to resolve them in any area of life. They will teach love and not fear.

One resistance to exploring what fears might be creating our outer conditions is that we may fear our own blame. To admit that we create our external conditions seems to imply that we are to blame or at fault for any mistakes we have made. It is a misinterpretation to think that because we are totally responsible for the creation of our lives that we are therefore to blame for the errors we have made. Blame implies sin and guilt which implies punishment. However, error implies correction without judgment which implies learning and teaching. Though we are responsible for, and the creators of, our errors, we are not to blame for them. We have not sinned and we do not need to be punished. We have only made the error of choosing fear instead of love. This requires recognition and correction.

We may inwardly feel that any financial lack is a punishment for past unloving acts or thoughts. Whether we have articulated it to ourselves or not, we may feel that we live in a punitive Universe. This belief, that there is a God who will punish us for our sins, is strengthened by many of our traditional churches, though not necessarily by the teachings they represent. Rather than believing we were created in the image of a nonjudgmental and loving God, we have created a God in our own judgmental and condemning image.

If we believe in the unholy trinity of sin, guilt, and punishment, the concept that we are creating our lives, including our "mistakes," will generate greater fear and sabotage our efforts at self-understanding. Realizing that errors and mistakes are part of any learning process allows us to view these mistakes, no matter how painful they may be, as part of a growing process that is both necessary and normal. Thus, we can view ourselves as growing children who need to be lovingly taught. Except in rare instances, we have not yet seen the mature adult of our species.

Many people are beginning to accept the concept that our inner world may affect, if not actually create, our outer world. This thought-form is beginning to express itself in many ways; for example, in the idea that if you pursue what you love in your job or career, the money will follow. However, many of us know of situations where people, perhaps even ourselves, were pursuing a business or a career that we loved and the money did not follow. Now, perhaps it could be argued that these people must not have *really* loved what they were doing and that is why the money did not follow. But perhaps another explanation is possible.

If we truly love our work we will be successful in it per se, but not necessarily always manifest financial abundance from this work. The love of our work will create abundance in other areas such as quality, satisfaction, service to others, and personal growth. In any area where we fear lack, we may manifest lack in that area. Or we may fearfully create excess. The amount of money we create in our lives is not regulated by our attitudes or feelings concerning our work, but rather by our attitudes and feelings concerning money and our own level of prosperity.

This accounts for the fact that people may be doing what they love but the money does not follow and conversely, that people may do things they dislike and still become wealthy.

These thoughts and emotions exist on a continuum from "poverty consciousness" to "prosperity consciousness." It stretches from perceiving the world as a place of lack to seeing it as a place of abundance. This is not to say that the wealthiest people are those that are clearest in their perception regarding money and abundance. People often are financially well off but still exist within a "poverty consciousness," believing themselves to have attained their needed resources from a limited and ever dwindling supply. Correspondingly, many people may exist on limited means, yet may operate from a "prosperity consciousness," believing themselves to have an abundance for their needs. This may seem to be a contradiction but really it is not.

If we are doing what we love but are still coming from a fear of lack of money, rather than a trust of abundance, we may or may not create financial prosperity or financial poverty in our lives. This will depend on how we have envisioned or imagined ourselves and our lives to be in regards to our finances. The basis for this imagining or envisioning can be based on either fear or trust. We are always creating out of our deepest thoughts and feelings. Say, for instance, we fear or believe the Universe to be a place of lack, although within these fears, we also hold an image or vision of ourselves as having a level of financial prosperity within this Universe of lack. In this case, we will probably achieve financial prosperity, yet still remain fearful and operate from a fear of lack. If within our view of a Universe of lack we envision ourselves as never having enough money or just barely enough, we will be financially impoverished or just getting by while existing within our perception of a Universe of lack.

Correspondingly, prosperity consciousness is not always manifested by an excess of money. True prosperity consciousness is an understanding that the Universe always offers us abundance and that we are able to manifest this abundance through our thoughts, emotions, and will. We will manifest prosperity consciousness no matter what financial level we have attained. We will understand we will all have an abundance in relation to our needs no matter what financial level we are on. We will no longer live, and manifest, fearing there is not enough; enough money, enough love, enough time, enough energy, enough opportunities. We will trust that we will be given what we need in all these areas and our rung on the financial ladder will become of little importance as we pursue our mission. What can an abundance of money offer when the ability to awaken and heal ourselves and others is available to us? This awakening and healing will actually offer us the peace that we mistakenly thought our money could buy.

The mind is the most powerful device for change that exists.

If we have begun to believe and have faith in the total benevolence of our Universe, we will also understand that such a Universe always expresses abundance and never lack. The material lack we see is only the expression of our fears that there is not enough. Since fear is the dominant thought-form on the planet, the physical "real" world reflects a Universe that appears to be a place of lack. This reflection in the physical world then solidifies and justifies this perception.

This is why cycles of poverty (and cycles of prosperity) are hard to break. If we are born into poverty and everything about our environment reflects poverty and lack back to us, it is almost certain that we will view the Universe as a place of lack. In addition, it will be very difficult for us to form and hold an image of ourselves as living in abundance and prosperity. One or both of these perceptions must be changed before the cycle can be broken.

It is not only those of us who were born into an environment of financial poverty that have been programmed to view the world as a place of lack or to manifest abundance in poverty consciousness. Up to this stage of our species' evolution, most of us have perceived the Universe as a place of lack. We are told by our parents, our community, and our society that lack and poverty are inherent and unchangeable conditions of the world, even if many of us are able to manifest abundance within this Universe. We are constantly warned that there may not be enough for our needs so we must be sure that deprivation never catches up with us. Our own parents' attitudes about money and prosperity, whether they were spoken or just emoted in our homes, were transferred to us. These attitudes are then reinforced by our community and society.

Many of our religious teachings serve to remind us that the Universe is an abundant place and that we can trust that all our needs will be provided for. Many people are willing to accept this but only in a limited fashion. They are ready to trust God, but not explicitly and entirely. Fear remains to dictate that we had better trust mainly in our own efforts, just in case God fails, or worse yet, does not really care or exist.

Our perception of, and belief in, a Universe of lack is not only manifested in our financial lives. We may believe that there is not enough time, money, energy, or opportunities in our lives. One of the most common, and emotionally destructive fears is that there is not enough love. Since many of us have come from families that were emotionally and/or spiritually impoverished, it is understandable how this perception was formed. As we observed our family relationships, our outer world seemed to represent a lack of real love, so we decided that there might be a limited supply of love in the Universe. We did not understand that it was the thought-form of the species, rather than something inherent in the Universe, that caused this condition of lack. We misinterpreted this lack as an unalterable law of the Universe. The correct Universal law is that the material world is a reflection created by our thoughts, emotions, and will. This law in itself is unalterable but the physical world is easily altered as we change our thoughts and emotions. We can change our "luck" or our financial condition by altering our thoughts and feelings. The mind is the most powerful device for change that exists.

The fear that there is not enough love is prevalent everywhere. In many ways this fear underlies all other fears. In our personal lives it manifests itself in many ways. We may become jealous or limit our relationships, fearing that human beings only have so much love to give. We may think ourselves unlovable and create a lonely, isolated world. We may fear we are too old, too busy, or too unloving to be granted love from the limited and greatly diminished allotment that each person has available to them. We may feel we have already met, and then lost, most of the people who will ever love us.

This fear of lack of love often manifests itself clearly in our perception that there is a limited number of people we can happily marry (many people fear there is only one). If we perceive some condition as depriving us of this limited number (loss of a mate, not enough potential mates of the correct age, interests, or financial status), our fear that we may never find a loving mate begins to surface and dominate. If we believe in a random Universe, we may feel we will not be lucky in finding a loving mate. If we view a punitive Universe, we may feel undeserving and punished for past unloving acts. This fear then creates a physical Universe lacking in a loving mate. Then we interpret this physical lack as proof of our fears. We have forgotten that a benevolent Universe would not bestow within us a deepseated longing that could never be satisfied or satisfied once and then lost forever. We have forgotten that there is an abundance of love in the Universe, in all and any form we choose to create it.

However, we must resolve our fears in any area before our belief and faith in an abundant Universe can become the dominant force in our thoughts and emotions. Not all of the fear has to disappear, but love and trust must replace fear as the *dominant* emotions. Once they have, our outer lives will begin to represent, not our fears and belief in scarcity, but rather our trust and awareness that we exist within a loving and abundant Universe, where all that we need is provided.

Once this transition has been made in our mental and emotional worlds, our relationship to money and prosperity will have made a crucial and profound change. We might think that this change will lead to greater wealth and financial prosperity. This is not necessarily the case. As we begin to perceive the Universe as a place of abundance we will understand that we have what we need (money, health, friendship, meaningful work, and love) and that we no longer need to worry about how much money we have. Now we no longer need to feel driven to accumulate and hoard money for eventual periods of lack, since we understand these will not occur, unless our fears create them. If periods of lack occur, they can be reversed, not by scrambling for more money, but by adjusting our thinking and feeling from fear to love and trust. The derivative of affluence is "to flow." The derivative of wealth is "well-being." We can always create "affluence" and "wealth" in our lives.

It may seem to follow that we should never save money or that we should give all excess funds to charity. However, we can provide for our future in a balanced and trusting manner, knowing that we will be guided, if we choose to open to our inner guidance, as to what funds we should use or reserve for ourselves and which ones are to be used to help others. This inner guidance, coupled with the knowledge of an abundant, benevolent Universe, will provide for our present and future needs. Which is not to say that we do not need to work or strive to improve or maintain our financial condition, it only means that we do not need to do so fearfully.

The concept that spiritual seeking involves the sacrifice of all the material things we desire has caused resistance

Nor does this mean that we must sacrifice all the material things we desire. It only means that we must not make them our idols. The concept that spiritual seeking involves the sacrifice of all the material things we desire has caused resistance in many of us. We are never asked to sacrifice anything that could bring us peace. A benevolent Universe will grant us our heart's desires and the peace of mind to truly enjoy using them if we keep them in their proper perspective, as a means rather than an end. These material objects—homes, cars, boats, furniture, etc.—are only props to be used in our ongoing function of teaching and learning love. They have no intrinsic value in themselves. The real sacrifice that usually occurs in life is to view ourselves and others simply as egos and bodies, thereby sacrificing the understanding that we are each divine miracle workers.

It could be argued that this comforting view of the Universe would encourage us to lead a life of idle self-indulgence, waiting for the Universe to provide all of our needs. But, our will, attention, *and* energy must also be extended. As we begin to accept that certain laws regarding our prosperity may be in operation, this awareness will also lead us to understand that we were not placed here simply to gratify our egos and bodies or placate our fears. This is why money alone can never offer peace of mind. We will understand that we have a specific mission. We will understand that we will be guided to a business, job, or calling that will not only bring us joy but will also involve service to others.

Resolving our fears, beginning to understand that the Universe is a place of abundance, and that learning and teaching love is our true purpose, does not determine which financial bracket we will fall into. Whether we become a millionaire or make a modest living will no longer be relevant for we will have begun to understand that we are being given what we need. If we are given financial abundance, then there must be a reason and purpose for it. If we are given only what we need to meet our commitments, and no excess, then our mission will not require any excess money, only our time and energy, in order to manifest itself. Of course our ego, with its desires and fears, will attempt to undermine the concept that our level on the financial ladder is irrelevant and that our needs will be provided for at whichever rung is most appropriate for us. The resolution of our fears appears as a direct threat to our ego, since they are its basis. Since we have been trained to associate our self-worth with the amount of money we make and/or amass, it is difficult to break this training. Our egos shout, the more we make, the better we are, chiming in with the chorus of our society.

When we believe in a random or punitive Universe, we feel the more assets we have the safer we are from harm or deprivation. But in a benevolent Universe, we can release our fears and we will always be provided for sufficiently. No harm will befall us. Things may happen that cause us emotional, physical, or financial pain, but though they are painful, they do not need to be interpreted as harmful or negative. These painful events are not chance happenings, but important and necessary lessons to help us learn and grow. There is no need to protect ourselves from these lessons. It is impossible to do so.

In addition to our vision or image of ourselves in regard to our financial status, our human will comes into play. Many books on how to become wealthier accurately lead the reader to the realization that our financial condition can be improved by willing it so. Many wealthy and/or powerful people have, either consciously or unconsciously, understood this. They have directed their powerful desires towards amassing fortunes and/or power and have coupled this with their image of themselves as wealthy or powerful people. They may still live in fear. They may love or hate their work. They may be ethical or unethical. But they have manifested wealth and power through their desires, their human will, and their ability to image. They have focused these three powerful human forces on a goal and have created it. However, if we manifest things only from our human desires and will, we may become wealthy but we will not be balanced and at peace. This is why "successful" people seem to manifest what they want (wealth, power, fame, accomplishments), but seldom do they seem peaceful. Peace assumes a condition of feeling as though what we are doing is what we are meant to do, that we are in some way on the right track and working towards our goal or mission in life. Since the human will and desires are creations of our ego, not of our Higher Self, they will never lead us towards our true mission and therefore to peace. Asserting our human will, emotions, and thoughts will give us what our egos desire but the attainment of these desires will not necessarily bring us the peace and fulfillment that we consciously or unconsciously seek.

This is why we always have a sense of restlessness, a sense that this is not quite it. We are always thinking that we will really feel at peace when we get that next promotion, make that sum of money, marry the right person or divorce the wrong one, move to the next house, change our career or job, have the next child, and on and on and on. This restlessness is both a safety device and a homing beacon. As a safety device, it assures us that we will never stop at a false purpose or squander our energy and time indefinitely on an illusion. We will become restless and keep seeking the next goal, thinking that perhaps this might give us peace. This restlessness will continue till we have tried all the alternatives, all the alluring and yet somehow empty pursuits. For a period, we will continue to seek for this peace outside ourselves. We will continue to walk down deadend trails. Each false lead, each step, is necessary so that we will become free of its sway. Each step down the deadend trails of illusion will be a mixture of pleasure and pain but offer little joy or peace. The pleasure is in the temporary gratification of the ego or physical senses. The pain is the result of discovering that what we thought would bring us lasting happiness and peace was only an illusion and has offered us neither.

This pain is a safety mechanism to remind us that we are more than egos within physical bodies and that the gratification of either will never satisfy the longings of our Higher Self. Each step seems to lead farther and farther from the joy and peace we seek, though in reality, each step leads closer, for the sooner we understand the illusions at the end of each trail, the sooner we can be free of them. We are always exactly where we need to be. Our free will allows us limitless choices. No matter how far off the path we may appear, we are always headed Home. The more we can share with each other the deadend paths we have been down, the more we can help lead each other more quickly there.

In the early stages of our spiritual development we seek gratification through the physical senses—sex, drugs, alcohol, food and drink. As we evolve further, we seek gratification through the ego, through jobs, marriages, possessions, power, and accomplishments. It is only in the later stages of our spiritual development that we begin to understand these illusions and to become aware of who we really are, Divine Beings who are able to bring the miracle of unconditional love into every relationship and situation. We begin to seek peace through our relationships, our service to others, and our own inner search. We stop seeking satisfaction primarily from things outside ourselves and turn within. By doing this, we have finally turned off all the deadend trails and turned down the main road that will lead us Home.

It is in this way that the constant restlessness acts as a homing beacon. It will keep calling us until we come Home. It is similar to being sent on a journey to a sacred temple within a great city with a special and sacred mission to accomplish. On the journey we become distracted and captivated by all the events and sensations of the city. After awhile we fall under their influence and forget where we came from or why we were sent, totally immersing ourselves in the alluring surroundings. But somewhere in the back of our consciousness a nagging voice reminds us that these sensations and distractions are not really why we are here. For a long time we may ignore this voice. Gradually, we begin to hear this voice but for awhile longer we do not choose to listen and therefore we still cannot remember our true purpose. We just know that what we are doing is not it. Here the search intensifies as we begin to look for something different, though we are not yet sure what. We begin to search for a better way. Eventually, the search will lead us back to our true mission and the road Home. In time we will remember who sent us and why.

As we begin to seek a better way and turn within for our fulfillment, we ask our Higher Self, our Divine Self, to participate, and eventually dominate, in our actions and decision making, whether we are aware of it or not. For some people this seems equivalent to the religious concept of turning our lives over to God (Spirit, Christ, Divine Guidance, etc.). In religious terms this is often expressed as "Father, not my will, but Yours, be done." In our modern Western culture we may find this personally insulting; we have been trained that the highest level we can ascend to is one of total personal control of our thoughts, emotions, actions, and lives. Indeed, our heroes and leaders are those within the culture who have been most successful at manifesting their desires through their *human* will. The state of the planet in general, and the individual lives of most people in particular, is proof enough that the existing use of the human will, fueled by our ego's emotions and desires, is unsuccessful in creating the peaceful and joyous world we are all seeking.

We are always exactly where we need to be. Our free will allows us limitless choices.

Turning our wills over to the guidance of our Higher Self and asking our Spirit to guide us, is a much clearer and more peaceful process of existing. However, several misunderstandings and misinterpretations may get in the way of using this process. The idea of turning our will over to anyone or anything other than ourselves is perceived as dangerous and frightening. It may also be perceived as involving self-sacrifice and based on weakness rather than strength. Having believed we created ourselves or were created through a random gathering of molecules, we have come to believe that there is no greater or clearer authority than our ego and human will.

If we begin to understand that we are actually spiritual beings, much greater than just our egos, we will understand that we have given control of our lives to an illusion, not to our true selves. We feel an internal restlessness *because* we have turned control over to someone or something that is not truly who we are. We have mistaken the desires and fears of this ego as ourselves and have sought its advice and direction in our lives. Our constant unrest and pain derives from the fact that our ego, being only the fearful illusion of who we really are, can never provide us the needed guidance and answers to direct us to our goal of peace and joy.

By asking for guidance to manifest the teaching and the learning of love in all situations in our lives, we are not seeking advice from, nor giving control to some Divine Being outside ourselves, but rather to one that is also within ourselves. We are asking that our true nature, which is Love, manifest itself in our lives. We are not giving away control, but rather taking it back from the illusion of ourselves that we gave it to a long time ago.

Until our True Self, our Higher Self, which seeks only to give and receive love, is given the permission and encouragement to manifest its will through us, our lives will remain a painful reflection of our human fears. We will never truly be at peace until we start on a more direct road Home, until we are doing what we were sent here to do, to express love.

We may still be at the beginning of this road, but once we have begun to accept that peace and fulfillment may exist within us, we are heading Home. And every step down this road, though some may involve pain, confusion, searching, and effort, will become one step closer to Home. Because of this, each step will lead to greater and greater peace and joy.

Each step will come at the proper time in our lives. There will be no need to rush ahead to the next step before we have mastered and integrated the lessons presented to us now. We will never be given more than we are totally prepared to handle; each step contains trials and tribulations as well as the strength to handle them. As we begin to turn within, towards our own Divine Nature, and towards love and service to others, each step will offer us wholeness and peace.

Listed below are commonly
accepted principles and their underlying
fears. Score yourself on a scale from 1 to
10 to see how your present thoughts
and emotions are formed by these
principles and fears.

Accepted Principles

1. There is a limited supply of money available.

2. Lack is a permanent and unchangeable condition in the Universe.

3. External conditions (recession, educational level, age, our jobs, debts, luck) control our financial destiny.

4. Money can keep us safe from many forms of harm and discomfort.

5. The more money people have, the less fear they have regarding money.

6. If we do what we love, the money will follow.

7. If we work hard, we will have enough money.

8. If we work hard *and* with integrity, we will have enough money.

9. You have to have money to make money.

10. Money is the root of all evil.

11. A spiritual or socially committed life is a life of poverty or limited financial resources.

12. People respect you more if you have attained a certain financial status.

Fears Underlying
Accepted Principles

1 I fear that the Universe is a place of lack with a limited supply of money. _____

2 I fear that I do not have and/or will not have enough money. _____

3 I fear that I am not in control of my financial condition. _____

4 I fear outside forces and situations are in control of my financial condition. _____

5 I fear I may be to blame for painful conditions in my life, including my financial condition. _____

6 I fear I am or may be punished with financial lack for my past acts, thoughts, or emotions. _____

7 I fear that even a good financial condition can deteriorate at any time without my ability to stop or change it. _____

8 I fear people may not respect me unless I attain a certain financial level. _____

9 I fear, though I have enough money now, I will not have enough in the future. _____

10 I fear that if I have too much money I am being greedy, selfish, and materialistic. _____

11 I fear that there are only a few sources of money available to me and if I lose any of them, it will be hard or impossible to replace them. _____

Each step will come at the proper time in our lives.

There are no failures. Everything in life is a learning experience designed for our greatest balanced growth and development. What appear to be failures are really gifts, which allow us to recognize and release all our fears and blocks so that we may create joy and success in similar situations in the future. These gifts are lessons we have failed to learn, so that where, previously, we made a faulty choice, we are now given the opportunity to choose again (*Course*, text, pg. 620).

The Gift of Failure

The fear of failure is one of the most common and powerful forces in the workplace. Though often disguised as a drive to achieve or excel, this fear is insidious in its ability to rob our peace of mind and upset our lives. It is both an inhibitor of and motivator for human action. As an inhibitor, the fear of failure often hinders us from attempting many worthy endeavors. On other occasions, this same fear dominates our decision-making process and motivates us to action in an attempt to placate it.

Two common misperceptions or misinterpretations lie at the root of this fear. One misperception is that a failure is something negative, that things would have been better if it had not happened. This often leads to the second misperception, that a failure in our endeavors may indicate a failure in us as a person.

As we begin to understand the true purpose of failures, the fear of them begins to lose its hold on us and to recede. In a benevolent Universe, every situation in our lives is a gift, though we may fail to recognize it as such. Failures are often our greatest gifts in that they may serve to bring our fears into sharp and painful focus. The failures do not necessarily validate our fears, as is often our interpretation, but only serve to uncover them so that we may realize they are inappropriate. We can then begin to release them so that we no longer need these painful gifts. We can begin to understand that our Universe is safe.

In addition to these inappropriate fears, our commercially-oriented society so strongly affects our thinking, that we directly link our success in our career or business endeavors with our success as a person. We have forgotten our own inherent self-worth. In reverse thinking (wrong-mindedness), our egos have convinced us that we are much less than we really are. By using the ego's standards, we have come to measure our value by what we accomplish and possess. We have temporarily forgotten that we are much greater than this. We have forgotten that we are divine beings capable of creating miracles of love in every situation, transforming all those involved.

No one is immune to the fear of failing; all of us have failed and misinterpreted its meaning. The experience of failing is painful. However, it is this pain that can initiate a search for its sources. We can begin to realize that to fail in an endeavor in no way indicates our failure as a person. Nor does it necessarily have to upset our peace of mind or self-esteem, unless we allow it to. The failure either points to a lack of knowledge in regards to the realities of the endeavor or to inner fears that prevent us from creating success. Or both. In either case, correction, not condemnation, is the appropriate response.

In the truest sense there really are no failures, they are always just opportunities to learn and grow and to discover and release our fears. They are opportunities to add to our knowledge concerning the endeavor so that we will be better equipped to create the outcome we desire the next time around. All knowledge, especially self-knowledge, is of use and value to us, no matter how painful it may initially appear.

As we begin to recognize these different layers of fears, they begin to lose their hold on us. If we begin to remember that the Universe always serves us in a loving manner and that often our most painful situations are our best opportunities for growth, we will perceive that what may appear as punishments or failures are really our most needed lessons. We often misread a situation as a "failure" or a punishment when actually it is a learning tool. In Chinese, the word for disaster and opportunity is the same.

Experience, in and of itself, does not really establish wisdom. How often have we continued to re-create the same painful "failures," seemingly learning nothing from our earlier experiences. Rather, it is the correct understanding and interpretation of our experiences that builds a foundation of wise judgment, allowing us to create the outcomes of our choice, rather than having the outcomes twisted by our fears.

In its simplest form, a failure may just indicate that we lacked sufficient information to create the desired outcome. We may have misjudged the task at hand; the marketplace; the scope of the project; the amount of time, money, and energy needed; other people's reactions; etc. This type of failure may not indicate the existence of any fears but rather, be evidence that more data is needed. (However, the lack of sufficient data may be the result of some fear.) These failures are usually not repeated and are easily corrected by applying our newly learned lessons and by being more diligent in the future. Usually our response to these failures is not as intense or emotional as our responses to the failures manufactured by our fears.

In Chinese, the word for disaster and opportunity is the same.

However, many, if not most failures, sprout from the seeds of our fears. If we will honestly review the different failures in our lives, we will often see that we made quite a few of the decisions that led to a particular failure based on fear. We fear we may not have enough money or work, so we jump into a job or business without thoroughly investigating it. We overlook possible problems or underestimate the requirements of an endeavor because we are afraid an honest evaluation will indicate that it may not be feasible. We commit to things because we are afraid to say no or fear admitting the task is beyond our abilities or our available time and energy. The results of an endeavor are often tainted by the original planning of the project which is all too often fear-based. These failures would seem to validate the fears when in reality their purpose is only to expose them.

If we begin to understand that situations in our lives are learning tools, we can become less attached to their outcome. This does not mean that we should not establish a preferred and planned outcome and then pursue it in a determined, persistent, and yet balanced manner. However, if we understand the true purpose of our endeavor, we can accept, though not desire or encourage, outcomes other than the ones we have planned. Even "failure" can be acceptable. We can then accept that despite our best efforts, failure may still result. If we are willing to learn whatever lessons about ourselves that this outcome has to offer, we can get on with our lives. We do not need to be negatively affected by the failure. We can ask ourselves, what gift does this failure have to offer? What fears caused us to bring about this failure? What can we learn about ourselves or the world from this?

Endeavors that appear to be failures measured by one set of standards, may actually be quite successful measured by another. Endeavors might be considered failures in terms of the "real world" because they have not met some criteria (profit, awards, promotion, peer acknowledgment, expected outcomes, etc.). However, they may be quite successful as defined by a more mature value system. If a situation is handled with high intent and honesty, with care and concern for the people involved, it may be successful in transforming the attitudes of these people, even though, on a "real world" basis, it appears a failure. It may have encouraged communication, growth, and love in those involved and on this essential basis, it was a success. In this key area we are always able to determine the success or failure of an endeavor, by choosing love or fear.

A failure may often unmask a basic life fear that is affecting us in many areas of our lives, not just our worklives. A failure that appears to be due to our overextending ourselves may reveal our fear of saying "no" or our need to please people. As we peel the layers back, this may reveal the fear that we must give everyone what they want from us or that our needs, and therefore we, are not as important as others. A failure based on our need to compete and achieve may reveal our fear of being "less" than others or our need to establish our self-worth through defeating others. All fears are fears regarding our self-worth which we have mistakenly connected to things, events, and people outside ourselves.

There will be a tremendous resistance to exploring what it is within ourselves that created a failure or painful outcome if we also fear our own self-blame. Blame and guilt are never appropriate. We have not sinned and are not in need of punishment (*Course*, text, p. 377). We have only erred and stand in need of correction. We need to search for and understand our own inner fears with the same dispassionate method that we would seek out a mistake in a computer program, for in many ways, they are very similar. Having located the error, we can understand the past events and present fears that created it and then go about correcting it so it no longer affects our decisions and actions.

Often, in order to avoid this inner search, we blame others for our failures. In this scenario, we project our own inappropriate blame and attack onto them. Once again, we have decided that we are the effect of our world, at its mercy, instead of being the cause and creator of it. On the physical plane, it may well seem that others had a major or minor part in our failure. But we need to ask ourselves why we have created this person and their fearful behavior in our life. This person is not in our life by accident. They have been sent with a lesson for us.

Failures, properly perceived, can create positive growth in a person. Misperceived, they can break a person's spirit and will. When we confront a failure or possible failure, many of our fears are triggered. We begin to imagine all the possible ramifications of the failure: the loss of others' esteem; the loss of money, time, and energy; and the problems created by the failure. We may begin to feel overwhelmed as each ramification triggers more and more fears. Indeed, it is the triggering of these fears, if we can understand and release them, that is the gift and the blessing of the failure. The purpose of the failure is to expose these fears. If we do not decide to confront and resolve them, we will instead desperately seek to placate them, and if this fails, we can become lost in panic, depression, anxiety, and/or hopelessness. The failure seems to confirm our deepest fears about ourselves. We tell ourselves that we are flawed for having failed and promise never to allow another such failure to recur. Or we may feel helpless to prevent them and drift into inactivity or hopelessness.

These fears often immobilize a person and cause them to avoid all situations that may entail any possibility of another failure. It can crush a person if they become convinced that all they can do is fail. Ironically, a person can also be propelled to great achievements by creating a stiff determination to avoid failure at all costs. In either case, the person is dominated by their fears.

We spend much of our lives worrying about things that never happen.

When fear is the basis for human achievement, we are tempted to believe that the fear is desirable and should be left as it is, perhaps even nurtured. This is similar to believing that since we are getting somewhere by crawling, why go through the process of learning to walk, with its inherent falls and bruises. Often, a constant stream of successes allows us to placate these fears so that they never become painful enough to confront. The successes or accomplishments are a narcotic that eases the pain so that we are never deeply motivated to cure the fear that is at the root of the pain. If we can accomplish when driven by our fears, imagine what we can do when we are free of these fears.

It is in this sense that a failure can be a great gift. It interrupts the narcotic effect of our successes and the pain floods in. If we misinterpret this pain, we will quickly strive for another success to ease it. Or it may overwhelm us, making us feel like a failure for as long as we allow it to. However, we can also seek to understand the failure within the context of a benevolent Universe, where everything is a gift.

Even if no failure has occurred, the fear of failure can cripple us and rob us of our peace of mind. But this does not have to be. To correct this, the first thing we can do is reexamine the things we feared most would happen and place them in their proper perspective. We spend much of our lives worrying about things that never happen. Even if a few do, we tend to greatly exaggerate the impact they will have on our lives. To become more at peace with a possible failure, imagine the ones we fear most really happening. Then we can walk ourselves through the subsequent events and work out the details of what to do and say if it really happened. We can consider how we would continue with our lives after the failure. We need to keep working with the possible scenarios until we feel we have thought through what would be the best response given the situation. If we do this, we will feel the fear start to lose its grip on us and realize that even if our worst fears come to be, we can survive and succeed in the future.

Many people avoid this process of visualizing their responses in the event of a much-feared failure because they feel this may actually bring the failure about or in some way show a weakness or lack of resolve. However, if the fear of failure is present, the best thing we can do is to make peace with the possible results so that the grasp the fear has over our thoughts, emotions, and actions can be lessened.

We are now ready to use the failure (or its fear) as a learning device to root out and explore all the various beliefs, perceptions, and interpretations about ourselves and the world that are the basis of the fear or that created the failure. Can the failure expose our fears so that they can be resolved (not placated) and found to be inappropriate? Can we begin to analyze the fears that have become so much a part of our thinking that they have faded into the background and are almost unnoticeable, though their effect on our lives is constant and profound?

At the heart of the fear of failing is the prevalent concept that our possessions, our accomplishments, and our successes are indicators of our value as a human being. If we are accomplished, if we make a lot of money, if we own a lot of things, if we do not fail in our endeavors, if we receive the acknowledgment of our peers and associates, then we are successful as people. However, success in our businesses, jobs, or careers does not indicate our success as a human being. Many people who are very successful in their businesses are failures in many other areas of their lives, especially in areas relating to human relationships, where how well we are learning as a human being can truly be measured. Conversely, many people who are not considered successful in their careers or businesses are very successful as human beings, though the world often convinces them otherwise. Success in business only indicates that we have learned how to succeed in that one area. It may indicate that we have conquered our fears in regards to business success and making money. It does not indicate whether we are successful or not as a total human being.

However, the illusion that it does is a powerful one. The world equates business and career success with personal success and honors the wealthy and accomplished. It bestows possessions and praise on those who have learned to succeed in business or career, and we have come to equate this praise and these possessions with success as a person. Since these business and career successes are rewarded on the physical plane, we seldom stop to question their value. If someone is making a large salary or quickly advancing in their job, it would appear that these rewards are confirmation that they are on the right track. In reality, it only confirms that they are on the right track in regards to the business or career area of their lives, which represents but one of many facets of their total being.

If we were to distill this fear of failure down to its essence, we would find that it is based on a misunderstanding or a forgetting of who we really are. We have come to define ourselves in terms of our ego and to see ourselves as separate entities whose outer boundaries are our skin. In the ego's standards, the world's standards, we are valued by our possessions, our accomplishments, and our ranking. Viewing itself as separate from all other egos, it needs these things to establish its worth as compared to other egos. Herein lies the basis for competition, dominance, jealousy, alienation, using others, and the many other illusions arising from the mistaken perception that we are not one, but separate.

This value system represents the degree to which we are out-of-balance in our perception of what is important in human endeavors. We have forgotten our goal of peace of mind and our purpose—to teach and learn love. We have temporarily made career and business success, with all its external rewards, our god. Success in human relationships though, is rewarded with a greater sense of peace, love, and connectedness to our fellow human beings. These rewards are offered internally to their recipients rather than being greeted externally with applause, trophies, or pay raises. There is no TV show called "The Lifestyles of the Balanced and Loving."

Using fear as a motivator in management is a common technique. Though accepted, it is not necessarily the best technique nor one that nurtures human growth. Though it may have limited positive results in the area of a person's behavior, it will have negative results on the person. By valuing objects and accomplishments more than people, motivation through fear (of failure, of disapproval, of firing) will cause imbalance and will not lead to peace of mind or the greatest use of a person's capabilities, which is the ultimate goal of management. The image of the successful but unhappy workaholic is a common one in the "real world" of business. Many accomplished people are so out of fear. We have come to believe that to spend sixty to eighty hours a week at work indicates the degree of commitment to one's job. Sometimes it does but more often it also indicates the degree to which we are avoiding all of the other areas of our lives: our families, our health, our spiritual development, our recreation. It may also indicate the degree to which we fear failure.

Fear-based accomplishments will not lead to peace of mind and a true sense of self-worth, life's greatest rewards. They will not lead us to our mission in life. As a matter of fact, seeking peace of mind and self-esteem through a fear-based pursuit of accomplishments and possessions assures that we will never attain them. If we can begin to eliminate the fears that motivate and control our actions, we will find that we accomplish just as much but with greater clarity and balance. With this greater clarity we will know what to accomplish and how to go about it, to the benefit of all involved. Our accomplishments will spread over many areas of our lives, rather than being concentrated in just one area. Instead of focusing mainly on the business and career areas of our lives, at the expense of our families, our bodies, and our spiritual development, we will arrive at a state of greater harmony and balance.

If we reduce fear as a motivator, we will not necessarily reduce either the quality or quantity of our accomplishments. We will, however, stop producing out of a mistaken sense of our lack of self-worth and produce instead from self-respect and out of true understanding as

There is no TV show called "The Lifestyles of the Balanced and Loving."

to who we are. We will be guided by love, not fear. The nature of these more balanced, love-motivated accomplishments will not only direct us towards our goal, peace of mind and clarity of purpose, but will create positive growth and change in everyone associated with our endeavors. Fear-based accomplishments often do just the opposite, creating stress and conflict within ourselves and those with whom we are associated. We may accomplish what we set out to do, but at a high cost in regard to human emotions and growth. If this is the case, we may have accomplished our objectives but failed at our true purpose, the teaching and learning of love. We will have suffered a success of means but a confusion of goals.

The stress and conflict created by fear-based accomplishments also blocks our inner knowing or intuition. At its purest level, intuition is divine inner guidance to the course of action that will promote the greatest development and growth for all involved. This guidance does not come from our reasoning, logical mind but from a much deeper part of our being. This intuition is often hard to hear and when heard, usually not given credibility by the logical world in which we live. Even if we are in touch with this inner knowing, it is often hard to implement it in our work. This intuition is given very little value in the business community. It is hard to imagine walking into a meeting and telling one's peers we have pursued a course of action because it felt right at an intuitive level. Actually, our peers have a right to ask for more of a reason than this. Decisions need to make sense both from the reasoning mind and to "feel" right from our intuition. That is, they need to work from an everyday, dollars and cents, bottomline level *and* from an intuitive, "it feels right to me to do this" level. If we make decisions totally from our rational mind, they can lack creativity, morality, and be disregarding the messages we are receiving at an intuitive level. If we make decisions totally from intuition, without gathering all the facts diligently first, we do not know if our intuition would have guided us differently after all these facts were in. The decision needs to feel right in our heads and in our hearts.

Getting in touch with this inner guidance, this intuitive feeling for the best course of action, is simple but not easy. It is not easy because messages from both our desires and our fears can be interpreted as messages from our higher intuitive centers. To be sure it is our inner knowing and guidance, and not our fears or desires we are hearing, we must make peace with both of these. We must be sure that our fears do not dominate our decision making and subsequent actions. Our decisions need to be based on our values and integrity, not on fears or external conditions.

Because they are even harder to identify, our ego and body desires will often dominate our thoughts and emotions. These desires are different from the higher prompting of our hearts. They are desires to possess, to dominate, to be publicly or privately praised, to defeat others, and in other ways have our physical appetites or egos gratified. Our need to rationalize what we desire will lead us to call these desires an "intuitive feeling" for what in reality is simply what our egos and/ or bodies desire to do. This is very subtle and unless we are truly at peace with any guidance we receive, even that which does not placate our fears or give us what we desire, we will hear the voices of our fears and desires as intuition.

Decisions need to make sense both from the reasoning mind and to "feel" right from our intuition.

Before we can even begin to use our inner knowing we must remove the blocks to our awareness of its presence. Stress, fear, conflict, and upset are all blocks to this tremendously powerful and accurate, yet subtle, decision-making tool. We will never hear our intuition if our fears speak louder or stress and fatigue have weakened our ability to hear the voice of our inner guidance. Fear of failure creates this and also propels us to a state of activity and busyness (business) so that we are too distracted to calmly and quietly hear our intuition. The truth is, that someone working forty hours a week and balancing the other parts of their life can be more effective than someone working out-of-balance for sixty hours a week.

From a balanced state we can more clearly analyze and evaluate situations and opportunities. We are more open to our innate sense of what will work. We have the ability to sit back and reflect on our actions rather than having to decide from a place of stress and fatigue. We can recognize a decision based on our higher intuition in that the more we contemplate its enactment, the more peaceful and joyous we feel.

As we come to understand—to remember—that who we are is much greater than our egos could ever imagine, we begin to correct our perception of ourselves and others. Instead of the painful and/or unfulfilling situations that are created by our egos and therefore by our fears and misperceptions, we begin to create the miracles we were sent to create. If we start to understand, or even just accept the possibility that we are spiritual as well as mental, emotional, and physical beings, we will understand that we have that ability to create miracles of love in every moment of our lives, in every situation, no matter how small or how significant, by striving to perceive the situation and all those involved, with unconditional love. Each situation in our lives was created with only that goal in mind—to teach and learn love. Having fulfilled this goal, the miracle, the natural (not supernatural) unifying and purifying outcome, has occurred. To the degree each person involved will allow, they will have been taught love through the situation. Therefore, they will have grown and begun to remember who they are, as much as is possible given their present level of awareness. The ability to successfully create these miracles in our lives is always under our control. We need only choose love rather than fear. In this most important area, we can always choose and control whether we will fail or succeed, in each and everything we undertake.

From a balanced state we can more clearly analyze and evaluate situations and opportunities.

All of this has nothing to do with possessions, accomplishments, money, or "success" by the world's standards. It has only to do with human transformation, with human thoughts and feelings. We are not separate "getting and doing machines," as the ego would have us believe. We are walking miracle workers who, like the mythical alchemists, are able to transform every mundane situation into a golden miracle and in doing so, transform each individual involved. What could the "real world" and our egos offer us that could be more fulfilling than this?

> **L**isted below are commonly
> accepted principles and their underlying
> fears. Score yourself on a scale from 1 to
> 10 to see how your present thoughts
> and emotions are formed by these
> principles and fears.

Accepted Principles

1 Failures are indicators of a lack of competence, intelligence, and / or luck. _____

2 A failure is negative, it is a loss, and it would have been better for us had it not happened. _____

3 A failure may indicate a major flaw in us as a person. _____

4 Successful people succeed. Only failures fail. _____

5 Failures invalidate our previous successes. _____

6 A failure indicates that the endeavor should not have been attempted in the first place. _____

7 If the endeavor does not lead to the expected outcome, it is a failure. _____

8 If the endeavor is unsuccessful as measured by financial or career standards, it is a failure. _____

9 Having once failed, we are tainted forever. _____

10 A failure indicates a downhill turn in our life and / or career. _____

11 Failure will prove right anyone who opposed the endeavor. _____

12 Our worth is in direct relationship to our successes and failures. _____

Fears Underlying Accepted Principles

1 I fear failures are punishments for flaws in my nature or for imperfect past acts, thoughts, or words. _____

2 I fear failures are indicators that my business or career has peaked and I am on a downhill slide. _____

3 I fear failures are proof that people who are successful are better and in some way different from me and I do not have what it takes to be successful. _____

4 I fear all my past accomplishments or successes were due to luck or are in some other way undeserved. A failure will penetrate the illusion that I am a successful person. _____

5 I fear people will not like, love, and/or respect me if I do not succeed. _____

6 I fear this failure is the beginning of a series of failures and it will be difficult for me to succeed again. _____

7 I fear God will be disappointed in me if I fail. _____

**Fear-based accomplishments
will not lead to peace of mind
and a true sense of self-worth,
life's greatest rewards.**

We have come to believe giving
means to sacrifice and lose
something. The world tells us
that what we have is diminished
if we give. Miracles remind us
that giving means getting and
expanding. Miracles bring more
love to both the receiver *and*
the giver and in doing so reverse
the laws of the world.

CHAPTER 6

Miracles & Missions in the Workplace

The masters were trying to decide where to hide the most powerful force in the Universe, the ability to create miracles, so that we would not discover it until we're mature enough not to misuse it. They talked about putting it at the bottom of the deepest ocean or at the top of the highest mountain. Finally, they came across the perfect hiding place: they would hide it within each of us, because that would be the last place we would think to look.

Everyone would like to create miracles in their lives. It is easy to think of such wonderful things we could create and pain we could relieve if only we were able to create miracles. We could resolve all conflicts in love and harmony, heal all sicknesses, create abundance, and transform all relationships into ones of love. As we begin to understand who we are and what a miracle is, we will understand that we can, indeed, create all these things. It is as natural as breathing.

In our everyday worklives we assume that we possess various capabilities, or "tools," to accomplish what we want. These capabilities include such things as our knowledge, our abilities, our determination and will, our ability to persuade others, and our intuitive feelings. These are all well-known "tools" that are at our disposal to be used to accomplish our goals. We use them every day, with varying degrees of success. Though we often acknowledge luck or fate as a wild-card factor, we assume these tools are, for the most part, what is available to us to accomplish our goals.

In addition to this, we have most often defined these goals in terms of work accomplishments and/or ego desires. We have decided that the goals that we are meant to accomplish are those assigned to us by our bosses, jobs, or companies as well as those which we pursue to fulfill our own desires and aspirations. We then use the tools that we have available (our will, knowledge, contacts, abilities) in pursuit of these goals.

There is, however, another set of goals, and their corresponding "tools," available to us. These other goals do not conflict with or invalidate the goals that we have accepted as part of our job or that we have determined to be personal objectives. Indeed, they make the accomplishment of these goals much easier. These goals, though more ephemeral than our business goals, overlay all our efforts and actions, in all parts of our lives, whether we are aware of it or not. These goals are the learning and teaching of love. The tools we are given to assist in their attainment are our love and the miracles it creates.

In previous chapters it has been proposed that our main, and perhaps, sole purpose on the planet is the learning and teaching of unconditional love. Another way this could be stated is that our main purpose is self-discovery. Since love is our true nature, our inheritance from our Creator, whose nature is also love, then to learn this, and in doing so teach it, is simply a remembering of who we really are. Forgiving is simply recognizing that we forgot. We are given a body, then, not as a pleasuring tool, but rather as a communication vehicle and a framework for developing our potential. In this chapter, we will explore the natural extension of love, miracles, and their application in what appears to be an everyday, mundane workplace.

Miracles do not really defy the laws of nature, though at times they may seem to, but they do defy the laws we have come to believe operate in the world. We have come to believe giving means to sacrifice and lose something. The world tells us that what we have is diminished if we give. Miracles remind us that giving means getting and expanding. Miracles bring more love to both the receiver *and* the giver and in doing so reverse the laws of the world (*Course,* text, p. 1). In truth, it is only through this giving that love can expand. We can only have more by giving more. This is why life is "for giving."

We have come to believe we can only exert a limited control over our lives by the use of our will, desires, and personal power. Miracles remind us that we can create our lives totally through our love. The outcome of all situations are under our control if we offer each of them the miracles only love can bring. We have come to believe we are only bodies and egos, limited and defined. Miracles remind us we are limitless.

A miracle is anything and everything that comes from love.

Before proceeding, a definition of miracles is required, along with an understanding of some of their key principles. The most commonly accepted definition of miracles, that of supernatural acts created by supernaturally-powerful beings, is not what is intended here. Resistance to, and perhaps rejection of, the possibility of the existence of miracles will be the most likely response if miracles are interpreted as supernatural or unnatural acts. Their creation will seem unattainable if they are credited to the world of nonphysical Divine Beings. They will engender fear if they are perceived as the creation of some sinister or random force. Miracles will be easily dismissed if they are perceived as feats of magic or illusion. Any of these responses are understandable given our existing definition or interpretation of miracles.

However, here a reinterpretation is offered. A miracle is anything and everything that comes from love, unconditional love. Miracles are all expressions of love and all expressions of love are miracles (*Course,* text, p. 1). They are simply acts of love that we might never otherwise term as miracles, though occasionally their results may appear so incredible as to be considered "miraculous." Miracles seem rare or nonexistent only because we have misunderstood what they are and are struggling in an unnatural state in which our true nature is still hidden and therefore not able to express itself through miracles.

This, then, is a reinterpretation of miracles and some of the principles under which they operate. Their application in our worklives is no less viable than in any other area of our lives.

Every day, every hour, we are given the ability to create miracles in our lives. We are miracle workers, cocreators of our world and yet our egos have convinced us we are something much less than this. Many of these miracles appear as minor everyday events. A young child bumps into us and we respond with a loving pat on the head instead of the expected scowl. We take a moment to listen to the concerns of a friend or stranger and respond in a supportive, nonjudgmental manner. We signal for someone to pull ahead of us in traffic with a smile. We encourage love and forgiveness to express itself in a relationship previously dominated by resentment and conflict. We hug our children or show concern for our mate. We forgive a longheld hurt and feel free to love that person again, thereby turning an ancient hatred into a present love. All of these acts of love are miracles that teach love.

At first, these mundane situations may appear too ordinary to be classified as miracles but remember that a miracle is any act of unconditional love. It is often a small kindness that can have a lasting effect on our lives. We can all remember when a stranger or friend paid us a compliment or did us a kind deed. We can remember the sense of support and love we felt from this and recall how it increased our self-acceptance, causing us to love ourselves just a little more, if only for awhile. Perhaps we acted more loving towards others because of this. And because of what we did, they then acted more loving towards others they interacted with. And on and on, like a ripple in a lake when a stone has been cast. As the principles have stated, we do not know who or how our miracles will affect and these effects are often unobservable (*Course,* text, p. 3). But it is possible for a small act of love to trigger a major change in someone's life.

As with these smaller incidences, our more involved or ongoing situations at work (or elsewhere) offer us even more opportunities to create miracles. It may seem easier to allow the miracle to express itself by loving a stranger than someone you have been in conflict with for years. Since there is no hierarchy or order of difficulties in miracles,

miracles created in these more involved relationships are no more difficult or more important than those created from casual events (*Course,* text, p. 1). However, by their nature we have more opportunities to learn and teach love in these situations. Also, unlike onetime events, lessons in these ongoing relationships may involve different steps and stages, with various parts of the lesson to be mastered at each stage.

Perhaps you have an ongoing relationship with someone at work that is causing you conflict. Perhaps the person is not performing at an acceptable level, respecting you in your role, or is just difficult for you to get along with. Since these relationships continue over a period of time, it is easy for them to become hardened by judgment and resentment. We may decide the conflict is simply irresolvable and allow the situation to continually create conflict. We may attempt a more logical solution to the problem such as quitting, firing, transferring, or avoiding the person. However, we may be overlooking the most powerful implement for change we have and the only one that can assure success of resolving the conflict, the giving of our love and the miracles that it creates.

We can choose to love and forgive the "offending" person, by remembering, like us, they are simply a growing child asking for love. This does not mean liking the person or allowing poor quality or inadequate work or disrespectful behavior. We could choose to terminate the situation or not allow the unconscious behavior. This too can be healing if the correction comes from love, not judgment. We can lovingly stop disrespectful or attacking behavior in another by merging our self-respect with respect for others, by being both considerate and brave, empathetic yet self-respectful.

Since our love has dispersed our fears and clarified our thinking, we will feel guided towards the right action in any circumstance. This guidance will become clearer if we ask for it and as we seek a solution that encourages not only our growth, but that of the other person, even if it may be somewhat "painful." Choosing to love the other person ends the conflict for us. This is assured. The miracle has occurred.

There is no way to guarantee or predict what other miracles will occur from our act of love. Some may be observable, others not. The other person may not outwardly change at all or may change drastically or slowly. As the miracle has taught love, people witnessing the miracle may be moved by it and encouraged to do similarly in their lives. The other person or observers may begin to treat their family and acquaintances differently. In this way it may create undreamed of changes in the lives of people we have never met (*Course,* text, p. 4).

Often, though not always, the effects of these acts of love, these miracles, are observed not only through changes in human emotion and behavior. They may manifest on the physical plane, in a manner that can not be planned or anticipated. If love has been allowed to enter the situation, if only from one of its participants, the problem begins to correct itself, at least for this person. Perhaps after having chosen to love someone we have previously resented and judged, "miraculously" something occurs that balances the circumstances. Perhaps we, or they, are transferred, choose another job, or in some other way are removed from our contact. Perhaps their heart opens also and the conflict and stress dissolves. If we have chosen love we can be assured that no matter what occurs, it will be for our Highest Good.

We will be given all we need if we act from balance, integrity, and love.

The introduction of love into a problematic situation has more to do with reducing fear and increasing love and forgiveness within ourselves, rather than learning to love another person. The key issue is trust; trust that we will be given all we need if we act from balance, integrity, and love. Perhaps we are very fearful about our ability to successfully complete a task, or about being fired or otherwise losing a source of our income. Perhaps we are fearful about being passed over in a promotion or not advancing or excelling in our careers. In these fearful situations we are not loving and trusting ourselves or our world. Our fears testify to our belief in a random or punitive Universe where we are not safe and bad things can happen to us.

As in situations that involve forgiving others, the introduction of love and trust into these fearful circumstances will also create miracles.

We need only remember who we are and what our purpose is and that we are safe and loved in a totally benevolent Universe. If we release our fears and desires of the ego and body and ask that Divine Will express itself through us, it will be to the benefit of all involved. With the release of our fears, love is uncovered and miracles are created. As with other miracles, sometimes the results are simply that we are more at peace with situations that caused us fear in the past.

Just as often, though, the results are observable and tangible. Income is created from a source we had not expected. A task is accomplished with what seems to be a "miraculous" series of coincidences. Something that could have created a problem "all of a sudden" is resolved or is not as problematic as we feared. These are physical results the miracle has created.

Miracles have great power in them and are more than just one possible response among many. It would be easy to dismiss miracles as just the most loving response and different only because of this. However, miracles are much more than this. Miracles allow the Creator's will to work through us in the situation. This response is different from all others in that it is the only response that we were sent to offer and the only one that can offer peace. By responding from love we are responding from our true nature and allowing Divine Will, not our human will, to affect the results. In doing so we have allowed the most powerful force in the Universe to manifest itself. No matter how it may initially appear, it will offer us peace. All other responses will offer us conflict and illusion.

Mission

Aside from extending love in our everyday work situations, there is another way in which miracles are manifested in our careers, businesses, and lives. We can begin to seek our "mission" in our lives, which may or may not be the same as our career or jobs. Our mission, sometimes referred to as our calling or vocation, is something that is both assigned to us by our Creator and that we have chosen. It does not interrupt our free will.

We all have a mission that is shared *and* we each have a mission that is unique only to us. We share with everyone the mission of discovering our true nature and allowing this nature, love, to manifest all through our day. Our shared mission we have discussed throughout this book. It is our goal and purpose. It involves the constant seeking of our connection back to our Source, our Creator, and then the extension of His love to others. This mission is the same for everyone. It is the particular expression of this mission that is unique to each individual.

Each of us has a unique mission. At some level we may have always sensed this. We may have felt that there was something that we were meant to do, something we were sent here to do, but never quite sure what it was or whether we were actually doing it. We may have always been restless and wondered if what we were doing is what we were meant to do. Perhaps this restlessness has become more acute and we *know* that what we are doing is not why we were sent. Discovering our true mission is actually quite simple, though not necessarily easy. Our mission has several elements that will make it recognizable to us.

The most easily recognizable element of our mission on Earth is that it is something that we love to do. That can be a profession like computers, auto repair, medicine, teaching, psychotherapy, or selling things or it can be an interest like gardening, cooking, sailing, or sports. It is often parenting and nurturing of others. It may simply be talking and being with others. Whatever it is, and it may be several things, we will know it because we love to do it. It is what we would seek to do if nothing else interfered. We lose all sense of time and self when we are doing it. It offers us joy and peace.

For many of us, we may temporarily be so far removed from our mission that we think there is nothing that we really love to do. If this is the case begin to search with the knowledge that there is something for everyone. It may be something we loved as a child, teenager, or young adult, but have long abandoned as impractical or unworthy. It may be something that we love but does not fit our image of what our "mission" might be. It may involve something that "seems" unimportant like supporting and listening to others, playing with our kids, entertaining, coaching children, etc. For each of us there is something that we love and greatly desire to do. This desire is there because it is our mission and the mission is there because it is our desire. We all greatly desire and long to be accomplishing our mission.

The mission may be a line of work from which we earn our living. It may be a vocation or hobby. It may simply be something that we do around the other activities of our day, like listening to others or offering support. We will always be offered opportunities to express our mission as a loving God will always allow the innermost desires of his children to manifest themselves.

Another element to our mission is that it will offer service to others and fill a need in the world. Our mission is the crossroads between this great need and our innermost longing. Since our mission comes from our Creator and our Creator sent us here to help and serve each other, our mission will always involve assistance to others.

Realizing this may cause us to create a change in our activities. If we have been doing work that we love and feel it is our mission we may need to alter it so that it also serves the world's need. For instance, if we love to write TV screenplays, we may then decide to no longer work on TV shows that further solidify illusions but only on ones that express higher human values.

We share with everyone the mission of discovering our true nature.

As part of this mission we are encouraged to work within the environment that we feel most drawn to and that best supports us. For some this may be a big city, for others the suburbs and yet others a small village. Our daily life may also be of our choosing. We may feel drawn to work within a large corporation or bureaucracy. Others may feel drawn to a small business or to work alone at home. There is no "better" place or way. There are many missions, all of equal value.

Our mission is an ongoing process. If we are still alive, it is not complete. It is not one great work or accomplishment, but rather a lifetime's work. Whether it affects millions of people and is known to many or only affects a few family members, neighbors, and friends makes no difference. One is not better or more important than the other. It is only our egos that want certain recognition and observable results.

Our trust in a benevolent Universe and a loving Creator will be needed as we seek and manifest our mission. It may involve abandoning many years of experience and stability in a work that no longer has heart for you; it may just mean an adjustment in your existing activities. Trust and follow the path that has heart. You will be given all you need for its successful accomplishment. Guidance is no more than a simple prayer away. The guidance will always direct you towards peace, not fear. Trust and it will be revealed to you through the clearest desires of your heart. As the mythologist Joseph Campbell says, "Follow your bliss."

Discovering and working on our mission in life is more than just doing what we love most and serving others as we do it. When we are working at our mission, we have entered a state of grace in which the Creator's love is flowing clearly through us. Only here will we find our true happiness. *A Course In Miracles* states this well:

> Grace is the natural state of every Son of God. When he is not in a state of grace, he is out of his natural environment and does not function well. Everything he does becomes a strain, because he was not created for the environment he has made. He therefore cannot adapt to it, nor can he adapt it to him. There is no point in trying. A Son of God is happy only when he knows he is with God. That is the only environment in which he belongs. It is also the only environment that is worthy of him, because his own worth is beyond anything he can make (*Course*, text, p. 126).

Basic Principles of Miracles

(Reprinted, with slight alterations, from the fifty miracle principles
that begin the text of *A Course in Miracles*.)

•

One miracle is not harder or bigger than another.
There is no order of difficulty in miracles as they are all expressions
of love and therefore complete and whole.

•

Miracles are neither unnatural nor supernatural but rather natural expressions of love. Everything that comes from love is a miracle.

•

Miracles are habits, natural extensions during our day as we express our love. They should be involuntary and not under our conscious control as consciously selected miracles can be misguided by the ego.

•

When miracles are not occurring, something has gone wrong.

•

Everyone has the ability and the right to create miracles but in order to do this we must first resolve enough of our fears so that our true nature, love, begins to express itself. A purification of these fears is necessary first.

•

Miracles are healing because they fill a lack; they are performed by those who temporarily have more for those who temporarily have less.

•

Miracles are a kind of exchange. Like all expressions of love, the exchange reverses physical laws. More love is brought both to the giver and the receiver.

•

To consciously use a miracle to induce belief in their existence is a misunderstanding of their purpose.

•

Prayer is the medium of miracles. Prayer is not the beseeching and pleading to have what we want, but rather a means by which the created communicate with the Creator. Through this prayer, love is received from the Creator. Through our miracles love is then passed on to others.

•

Miracles are teaching devices and demonstrate that it is more blessed to give than receive. They simultaneously increase the strength of the giver and supply strength to the receiver.

•

A miracle is the greatest service you can render to another. By loving another unconditionally, you acknowledge and recognize their true nature and worth. In doing so, you remind both them and yourself of who we really are.

•

Miracles are natural signs of forgiveness. Through miracles you accept God's forgiveness by extending it to others.

•

Miracles should inspire gratitude, not awe. You should thank God for what you really are. The children of God are holy and miracles honor this holiness, which can be hidden but never lost.

•

Miracles honor you because you are lovable. They dispel illusions about yourself and perceive the light in you. By freeing your mind from the imprisonment of your illusions, they restore your sanity.

•

Miracles do not always have observable effects and their existence and value is not predicated on these effects.

•

Miracles release us from our false sense of isolation, deprivation, and lack. They unite us directly with others and result in true closeness.

•

Miracles may touch many people that we have never met or who were not directly involved in a situation. They may produce undreamed of changes in situations we are not aware of.

If You Want More

Hopefully this book has been of value in identifying and resolving the fears that are at play in our worklives. If you do not already perceive a benevolent Universe created by a loving God, I encourage you to experiment with the concepts contained in these chapters in your everyday worklives. Your own experience will then either nurture or undermine this perception.

The preceding chapters have not been a complete explanation of how all of life's pains and trials can be reconciled with the concept of a benevolent Universe. Subjects such as sickness and death have not been mentioned since they are not part of our everyday experiences in the workplace. The final chapter gives a more direct and detailed explanation of the possible operations of a benevolent Universe. When these painful events are reinterpreted, they may diminish some of the resistance to embracing such concepts.

Our mission is an ongoing process. If we are still alive, it is not complete.

If we were created by a Creator, we are always part of Him, as all creations are part of their creator. Perhaps we, as part of our Creator, can assist in orchestrating these events in our lives. As His energy is directed towards us, we take this energy and use it according to our own level of clarity. This is what is meant when we are told we were created in His image.

How Does The World Work?

This chapter presents three possible scenarios under which our Universe, and the everyday world we live in, may be operating. For the most part, people in the Western world believe, either consciously or unconsciously, in one of these models. Each model presents possible Universal laws that may be at work in our everyday lives.

This book assumes that one of the three is the most accurate and best reflects reality. It is not crucial that you agree with this particular model. You may agree with parts of it and strongly disagree with others. You may actively resist much of it. You may think it to be comforting, but not realistic given your observation of how the world is working. You may think that is exactly how the Universe is operating or that it is totally preposterous and invalid. None of this really matters for you to find value from this book (*Course,* workbook, p. 2).

The book has two parallel, but distinct, purposes. One purpose is to examine the emotions, and primarily the fears, that are operating in our worklives. The second purpose is to resolve these fears. No matter what your thoughts or feelings as to how the world is operating, this book will be of value to you in regards to the first purpose, that of examining your fears.

In regard to the second purpose, that of resolving and letting go of these fears, its effectiveness will depend on your world view. Given the random or punitive interpretation in two of the three world models, fears are valid and therefore their resolution is impossible. If we are at the mercy of good or bad luck, or if we can be punished for our past acts, then fear is appropriate and our world is not safe. Only the third model presents them as invalid and resolution as a natural consequence.

As you are presented with these scenarios, just allow yourself to agree or disagree, to judge or not, to accept or reject. After reading the book, try using some of the concepts presented in this model in your own everyday life and test their validity for yourself. It is not the intention of this book to convince you there is or is not a God or that, if there is, that He is punitive, indifferent, or loving. Its intention is to offer a reinterpretation of commonly perceived assumptions and to offer these on the field of reason. The test as to the validity of these reinterpretations will be your own experience. Through your own reason and experience you can then decide whether you want to alter your existing view or not (*Course,* workbook, p. 2).

The Three Main Views

Whether we realize it or not, everyone has decided how the Universe, and our world, operates. We may not have articulated this to ourselves or others. We may never have actually thought about or asked ourselves how the world is operating. We may never have viewed any issue from a Universal or global perspective. We may even think that the question of how the world is operating is beyond our understanding, of no interest to us, or unworthy of consideration. This does not matter. We all have a definite view as to how the world operates.

For the most part our world view, and the decisions that lead to our creation and acceptance of this view, was formed by both our experiences and by a transfer of ideas and emotions from the people and society we interact with. There is nothing complex in this concept. It is rather straightforward. A person brought up with love and abundance, and having had few painful experiences and little transfer of fearful thoughts, is more likely to decide that the Universe is an abundant, safe, and caring place. Someone who has experienced neglect or inattention, especially in the young formative years, may view the Universe as random and uncaring. Someone experiencing abuse and pain may have decided that the Universe is a place of pain, danger, and lack.

These are the "big picture" concepts that we have developed. There are also many specific components to our models. We may have decided that there is enough love in the world but not enough money or vice versa. We may have decided that good friendships are easy to create but that a fulfilling marriage is difficult or impossible for us to find. We may have decided that we can be fulfilled in our work but not in our family life or both. We may have decided that we are not worthy of success, happiness, or health or that it is our birthright. We may have decided that our pain is punishment for past "sins." The list goes on and on. All these decisions together, about each area of our lives, make up our view of how the Universe, and our world, are operating. They are the filters through which we perceive and interpret our world. Everyone has a model that they use; whether they know it, admit it, or want it.

In the Western world there seems to be three principle models that are accepted. This is not to say that there are not hybrids of these models or that we always operate under one model. Experiences, growth, and / or inner searching may cause us to alter or change our model. An examination of each of the three models will allow us to determine which model we have decided is operating in each of our lives.

Our first response when confronted with these three models may be to think that we easily know which one we believe in and operate under. However, it is best that we rethink our initial reaction to be sure that even though we may think, and wish we believed in a more positive model, we may in reality be living our lives with a deep-seated, but unrecognized and unarticulated, belief in a random or punitive world. If we feel fear, anger, depression, and / or resentment in any areas of our lives, it is testimony to our belief in this model and it is this we are teaching to ourselves and others.

1

No Creator / Random Universe and Planet

This model is very prevalent in the modern world since it fits the mechanistic/scientific view many of us have been taught and have come to believe. This model assumes that the fact that the Universe is operating in an orderly fashion is the result of a constant refinement through the ages of a coming together of random molecules. The molecules have evolved through a huge "hit or miss" process to their present complex and orderly state. There was no plan to this, no intelligent guidance, no purposeful direction. There was and is no Creator, no God. It all just came about as molecules bounced around together forming greater and greater complexities. The arrangements that "worked" remained and continued to grow. The arrangements that didn't "work" faded away. No one being created the Universe, or us, it just started a long time ago and continues today.

This view of the Universe also extends to the planet, even where human life on the planet is involved. For the most part, in the natural world things are working in an orderly fashion, given their continuing random refinement. Animal, plant, and natural worlds seem to operate in a working system that provides for more or less of a balance. Within these patterns of balance though, random events may occur. It may rain too much and flood, or not enough and cause a drought. Animals may overpopulate and die of starvation. Meteors may crash into the planet and cause an ice age. Volcanoes may erupt and change global weather patterns. There are orderly patterns but they can be disrupted by random, chance events, and thus the natural world is unpredictable and influenced by them.

This view is then applied to the area of human life. Since the planet and the Universe are operating in an unpredictable and random fashion, with no guiding or intelligent influence or purpose, our lives are also operating in this manner. What occurs in our lives is basically happening without plan. Though obviously we do have a certain level of control through our energy, actions, and will, this control can be upset at anytime by random events. Events are not part of some preordained destiny nor are they punishments or rewards from a Divine Being. They have no reason for being; they just happen. Some bring us pleasure, others pain.

Since there is some degree of order we can, by working hard to understand the various patterns, attempt to place ourselves in situations in which the odds for things happening as we would like are greatest. The more successful people are at doing this, the more they seem to get what they want, *unless* a random event interferes. Our task then is to try to understand as many of the patterns involved in different areas of our lives and interact with these patterns so that the odds are in our favor for a desirable outcome. Our goal and purpose is then to determine the patterns for making money, succeeding, accomplishing, making relationships happy, and keeping healthy and to make things work in our favor.

No matter how effective we are at this, and we can become very effective, we must always fear the random events that can erase all our best efforts. We can understand all the patterns of financial success and make these work for us, and still one day lose everything. We can do everything to keep ourselves and our loved ones healthy, and yet illness or accident can strike at anytime. We can understand the patterns in relationships and create a happy and balanced family life, and this too can be destroyed in one random event.

It often becomes exhausting trying to understand all the patterns and then trying to stack the odds in our favor by taking various courses of action. Not only are the patterns difficult to understand, having understood them we may not be financially, emotionally, or physically able to take the most favorable course of action. In addition, other people's desires to follow their best course may compete with ours and only one may prevail. And even if we have understood it and taken the most favorable course, all our efforts can be negated in one brief random event.

In this interpretation of the world, our lives have no purpose, no reason for being other than what we ourselves determine one to be. We are involved in a never-ending struggle to work the odds in our favor, yet always fearing devastating random events. We can be lucky or unlucky, clever or ignorant, successful or a failure. Setbacks or disasters can strike at anytime. Our control is limited and our safety is always uncertain and threatened. We are the effect of our world rather than being the cause of it. We have only ourselves to rely on to create a safe, happy, and successful life. Fear is appropriate in this Universe. Though we can placate fears by stacking the odds in our favor, resolution of all fears is impossible.

2

Created Universe / Punitive or Indifferent Planet

This paradigm is probably the most common one, at least in the Western world. The reason for this is twofold. First, it is the model that is taught in most traditional churches. In the past we have relied on the churches to explain to us how the world operated and this has been their answer. Second, since we, as a species, are still very judgmental, we tend to make the Universe, and our concept of our Creator, over in our image. Since we are often condemning and judgmental, we assume that our God must be also.

In this interpretation of the Universe, it is assumed that some highly intelligent Divine Being created the Universe. This Being, God, is referred to by many names and imaged in many forms. In this model it is not exactly clear why God created the Universe and the answer appears unknowable to us. The intelligence instilled into the Universe is apparent by the almost miraculous ways the various systems operate, from the smallest atom to the largest solar system. God is seen as the ultimate ruler and authority in this Universe, though some believe this authority can be challenged by the "devil" or Satan. The Universe is perceived as created according to a divine plan and its working out is not random, but is not necessarily preordained. The events we see are under Divine Control and the "negative" ones are often interpreted as punishments from the Creator.

It does not take a conscious belief in God to believe in a punitive world. We may believe that certain impersonal Universal laws mandate that rewards and punishments are connected to certain actions, thoughts, or even feelings. We reap what we sow, period. However, usually the belief in a punitive world also includes, though often unconsciously, the view of a punitive God. This is easy for many of us to accept since it agrees with many things we have been taught in our religions. Believing in the concept of sin, we therefore believe in its consequences, punishment. Since we believe others have "sinned" against us and that their punishment is justified, we must also believe this of ourselves, since we know we have also "sinned" against others. The concept of God as a stern, demanding, and punishing father figure is ingrained in the history and beliefs of the human race. Forgetting that we were told we were made in His image, we have made Him over in our image.

We may not feel that our God is really punitive and judgmental, but rather, that this Divine Being has set up the Universal laws of cause and effect. When we do something "wrong," something painful will happen to us, not because we have been judged and punished, but because we have reaped the natural consequences of these cause and effect laws. It is almost as if to say that the Creator, rather than punishing each person on an individual basis, has set into place certain impersonal laws that will provide for automatic punishment for each "sin." We may believe that God has nothing to do with our individual lives and only is concerned with larger projects such as creating universes. We may interpret this model as an indifferent God creating a punitive world.

We then believe that there is a God that loves us very much but cannot protect us from the punishments He has set in place. Like a loving but stern father, he allows us to suffer the consequences of our own actions. He may even need to reject us permanently (hell) if our transgressions are too great or our belief system not entirely correct or if we do not ask for His salvation in the proper fashion. In this case we believe in a loving God who has created a punitive Universe. Since it was His will to create this punitive Universe, He is both loving and punitive.

Our religions, using their interpretations of the Old and New Testaments, usually offer one of these interpretations of the Creator. They tell us we have one life, one chance, in which we are judged or scored as to our behavior, thoughts, and actions. If we score high enough we will go to heaven. If not, we are denied entrance to heaven or go to hell. No one really knows what the needed score is. Can we just be a basically good person or do we have to be almost a saint? Can we, as many religions teach, do anything we want and just ask to be saved in a certain fashion anytime before we die? And if we never ask to be saved, are we shut out of heaven, no matter what kind of life we have lived? Are God, and perhaps Jesus, judgmental scorekeepers, who never even reveal what a winning score is?

Religion can offer to placate these fears by telling us they know "the way" to insure our acceptance into heaven. However, fear is always appropriate in this model as we can never be quite sure of how we are doing. Even if we can be sure for ourselves, we must always fear eternal damnation for any loved ones who may not have followed the proper path. We may also believe that there is a devil who is always trying to lure us off this path, in subtle yet powerful ways. We teach our children this and tell them that they may live an eternity in horrendous pain unless they do certain things, most of which they do not yet understand. God is explained as a punitive or indifferent father figure who is separate from us and we must win His acceptance. We believe ourselves to be "sinners," tainted by original sin, who must correct and redeem ourselves in one short lifetime or else suffer eternally. With this model, fear is engendered and we teach a shame-based, God-fearing world.

Most psychotherapists would agree that a parent that was indifferent to their children or that threatened them with total and permanent rejection, would create a dysfunctional family. Perhaps it is our belief in this type of Divine father that has created much of our dysfunctional behavior and feelings.

3
Created Universe / Benevolent Creator and Planet

The third possible model of the Universe is one of a benevolent Creator establishing a totally benevolent Universe. Though most of us would like to believe in this world model, since it offers comfort and safety, it is the least common of all three views. The reason for this is because little in what we have experienced or observed *seems* to indicate that this is the accurate model. More correctly stated, what we have experienced and observed has programmed us to interpret these events in a certain way and these interpretations do not support the concept of a totally benevolent world or Creator. To believe in one seems to contradict what we observe and experience in our lives. How can a planet where death, disease, wars, accidents, pain, and conflict exist be totally benevolent and loving? Before discounting this view as naive, Pollyannaish, or invalid, read on.

This model assumes that a Divine Being, God, created the Universe. He created this Universe intelligently and with a purpose. Though it may remain as yet unclear as to why such a vast Universe was created, we can begin to make certain assumptions in regard to life on our particular planet.

This model also assumes that the Universe is a totally loving and safe environment, where nothing "bad" can ever happen to us no matter how it may appear otherwise. After it is reinterpreted, everything on the planet can be understood as a blessing or gift within a benevolent Universe. Nothing is an accident or punishment. This God is neither punitive nor judgmental, but like a loving parent He designs lessons to aid our growth and development. Some of these lessons are difficult and involve pain and are therefore perceived as bad luck or punishment. Like children we complain and think some lessons are too hard. This is only because we have misunderstood the meaning of pain. The rest of this chapter will examine some of the key aspects of life on earth and offer a reinterpretation of each using this model as a guide.

The Planet as a Schoolhouse

A random Universe assumes that the planet is a result of a huge hit or miss evolution. Belief in a punitive God assumes the planet is a testing field, battleground, or race course on which we all must score high enough in our allotted playing time (lifetime) to win the contest. Some will win, many will lose. One chance and that's it.

This third model however, assumes that the planet is a huge schoolroom, from which every student will eventually graduate. More accurately, the planet is a one room schoolhouse where both first graders and college students attend together. These grades in no way correspond to our physical age. A child may be in a much higher grade than their parent. A physical adult may be a spiritual child and vice versa. We all enter the planet at a certain grade level due to our work before this lifetime. It must also be remembered that all these differences are only temporary. In truth, all of the differences are illusions since we are always totally whole and complete but temporarily at different stages of remembering this.

This difference in spiritual awakening is why each day we can encounter or witness the most loving and the most selfish people, from the near animal to the near divine. Everyone must go through all the grades before they graduate. We are given many opportunities to work through all the grades and we can remain in any one grade for as long as we wish. Eventually though, we all progress, because everyone has a limited tolerance for pain (*Course,* text, p. 18).

The curriculum in this schoolhouse is set and we cannot change it. If students were allowed to establish the curriculum they might create a much easier one and it would not spur growth. However, our free will allows us to choose what we want to learn from this curriculum and when. We can set the pace of our learning. The curriculum has only one lesson to teach and that is unconditional love in all circumstances. We are here to learn love and in doing so, to teach it to others. More precisely, we are here to remove the blocks within us so as to be aware of love's presence. Love is our only lesson because that is who we are, it is our natural inheritance. All else is illusion. Total self-discovery of who we really are is therefore our real goal. Mastering this one lesson is the sole requirement for graduation (*Course,* text, introduction).

A first grader in this school would know little of love and therefore would mostly be involved in gratifying selfish physical appetites and be willing to use others to that end. Further along we may feel that others are here to satisfy any and all of our emotional needs (toxic parents, abusive partners, users, etc.). As we progress we begin to acknowledge other people's interests as well as our own. A sixth grader, for instance, might not really want to share with others but understands that he or she must do so anyway (analogous to selfish people who have learned to avoid harming others). Further along the path we begin to place others' interests equal to ours. For example, a teenager who begins to enjoy loving and giving to others and yet still enjoys receiving as well, not yet understanding the purpose and curriculum of the school (people who are openhearted and enjoy making others happy). In college we begin to become aware of our curriculum and are actively involved in learning it as quickly as possible. At this level we begin to realize that only through our love, service, and forgiveness will we experience the complete safety and peace we have always desired (i.e., people who have decided to follow their own inner guidance and devote much of their life's energy to serving others in whatever way they feel prompted to). Even graduate students, such as Jesus or Buddha, sometimes return to remind us of our goal and offer an example of life after graduation.

There should be no judgment attached to these different grades. We do not judge a little child because they can not drive or do calculus. Having been there ourselves, we can understand that the child will grow and that their behavior is appropriate for their age. This scenario is the same but we must think in terms of spiritual age and growth, not physical age. We all arrive on the planet in different grades. In any one family unit all different grades may be represented. This explains why children raised in the same family and circumstances often show varying degrees of ability to love. This also explains why some people who have been showered with love remain selfish and others who have known abuse or neglect somehow seem to rise above it and love others.

We are here to learn love and in doing so, to teach it to others.

Why the planet was set up like this is not yet clear. What is clear is that we, as spiritual beings incarnated in physical bodies become easily infatuated with and intoxicated by the pleasures and sensations of the physical plane. We develop egos and personalities and forget our more ephemeral spiritual nature. We perceive ourselves as separate entities with our skin as boundary.

We then begin to forget who we really are and why we were sent. It is this forgetting that causes various events in our lives to be painful. If we knew death was only a transition and only a temporary separation from loved ones it would be much easier to accept. If we understood our true spiritual nature and the abundance of love available to us we would not form the intense and painful attachments to others that are partially based in fear. If we knew attacking behavior was simply a twisted way of asking for love it would not hurt us. If we knew sickness and failure were opportunities to grow and uncover our fears and release them, they would not be so dreaded. The planet is in pain because we have forgotten who we are and turned our attention away from our source, Love, and our Creator, God.

However, the process is one of remembering, of trying many deadend streets (physical sensations, power, money, accomplishments, relationships) until we understand that it is only as we live in and express our spiritual nature that we will know peace. Until then we are not expressing who we really are and no one can be at peace when they do not understand who they are.

The reason for losing ourselves in the illusions of the physical plane, only to find ourselves after much searching, may have something to do with free will. Since the Universe is unlimited, free will is essential. Without free will, the Universe would be limited. Having free will, we are allowed to experiment with all manner of illusions. Only after we have fully experienced each one, to find out that none offer the satisfaction and peace of mind we had expected, can we be free of them forever. Their allure is gone. We will never make them our "god" again and assume our peace and safety reside with them.

No one
can be at peace
when they do not understand
who they are.

Everyone will eventually graduate from this schoolhouse because everyone will eventually remember who they are. To assist in this task of remembering, each person has been given certain homing beacons (i.e., restlessness and lack of inner peace) to serve as continual guidance. We are also outfitted with alerts (pain) that sound whenever we are heading in the wrong direction. Because of our free will, each of us may decide how long we want to remain in each grade. We can also skip grades; for example, when we are confronted with events that create a major impact in our lives. Again, there is no judgment involved and God has infinite patience with us. Eventually, our own pain and/or restlessness will propel us to learn the lessons we need to progress to the next grade. Earth is, after all, a school, not a resort or retirement home.

Human Beings as Energy Conduits

Even knowing that there may be an omnipotent God, it seems almost impossible that each and every event in every person's life could be an intelligent, conscious, and loving lesson. There just seem to be too many people, too many events, too many hours in the day. How could any mind, no matter how great, orchestrate such a world. Perhaps the concept that we are co-creators offers some clue.

If we were created by a Creator, we are always part of Him, as all creations are part of their creator. Perhaps we, as part of our Creator, can assist in orchestrating these events in our lives. As His energy is directed towards us, we take this energy and use it according to our own level of clarity. This is what is meant when we are told we were created in His image. We create our personal Universe just as God creates the Universe.

Imagine this Divine Energy pouring through each human being and as it does so it creates each person's life and external circumstances. It creates, affects, and molds the various situations, people, and conditions that are drawn to each person. As this energy passes through each human being, it is filtered through our thoughts, and more powerfully, through our emotions. The energy is affected by these filters; if they are clogged with fear they can warp and twist the energy until it is unrecognizable as anything even remotely associated with something divine.

By learning our lessons of love, we are cleaning these filters. The cleaner they are, the more clearly they allow the Divine Energy to flow through and create its purer expressions in our lives. In this sense, Divine Will, the Creator's Will, is always trying to express itself through us but with varying degrees of clarity. To desire to have this Will express itself through us, is not equivalent to turning our will over to another, which we may find personally insulting. It is rather the desire to so cleanse our filters that we more purely reflect the Divine Will and Energy that is constantly flowing through us. Our true will is always God's will. There is no conflict.

These filters have been created by our own lessons and experiences as well as by the transfer of other people's thoughts and emotions to us. Each person enters at a different grade, but our life's situations also have a great effect on them. Circumstances, especially those in our early years, can bring out our best or worst, can clarify the filters or darken them. The lesson in the schoolhouse is to observe the different thoughts, emotions, and decisions we have chosen that cloud our filters and to rechoose them, especially the unloving thoughts and emotions directed towards ourselves or others.

There are different filters for different parts of our lives. A person may have very dark filters in regard to intimate relationships and because of this they may create conflict and pain in their homes. This same person may have very clear filters in their worklife and be successful, or vice versa. Someone may be very clear in the area of friendship and feel they deserve, and that the world offers, good friends. This same person may believe a happy marriage is not possible for them, and in so believing they filter one out. If we want to know how clear our filters are in any part of our lives, if we want to know what thoughts, emotions, and decisions dominate any one area, we need only examine the outer expression of this area of our life. What we feel and think about any area of our lives, what kind of filter is in place there, will be expressed in our own personal Universe. We are cocreators. The planet is not full of suffering and pain because the Creator wills it so but because His creations are filtering out His energy and in doing so, creating their suffering. Because we have been given free will, we are free to create, or miscreate, as we choose.

Death as a Rest and Transition

Imagine a lifetime with no death. Imagine that we all lived forever and never died. More simply, imagine that we never slept, that days went on forever. What would it be like to never die or sleep? Though many people fear death, few of us would choose to live eternally.

It is understandable then, how there could be a compassionate and loving God who, within His benevolent Universe, allowed death to exist. Existing as we do with free will and creating painful lives in the earlier stages of our growth, we need death as a rest from these painful lives. Otherwise, we could become trapped in a painful life for a very long time.

Death is not just the release from painful lives, for indeed even people who have experienced little pain, die. Death is a way of prompting us to clarify our priorities and to make sure that we do not remain eternally along a deadend road. Death is also the final bell for that particular session in the schoolhouse. It is notification that the work we needed to do with that body is complete and so the body dies, whether we feel it is time or not. It is only a transition, not a final act. Without death we may tend to linger more slowly in learning our lessons.

Death is a way of prompting us to clarify our priorities.

The existence of death does not contradict or invalidate a benevolent Universe if death itself is a wonderful experience. Though so many of us have come to fear death, imagine if the freeing of the spirit from the physical body is the most enjoyable of all human experiences. Imagine that we are free of all pain and conflict and yet still conscious and whole, though no longer in a physical body. Imagine that we are reunited with all our loved ones that have preceded us in death and perhaps even loved ones we have not known in this lifetime. Imagine having the opportunities after death to nonjudgmentally review our lives and decide what areas still need work. If this is death, it could surely have been created by a loving Creator within a benevolent Universe.

However, what about us, the ones left behind in our bodies after a loved one dies, and experiencing the pain of missing them? Isn't this proof of a cruel Universe? Perhaps not. If we know they are safe and loved, then we experience no pain or fear for them. If we know our separation from them is only temporary and that a benevolent Universe will always provide us with all the love and companionship we are willing to open to, then we will not grieve as heavily for ourselves. We are always able to experience total joy in our lives at every moment, no matter what the outer circumstances.

With this scenario in mind, death would no longer be feared or used as proof that the world was random or punitive. The concern of how long we, or our loved ones, lived would not carry the weight it might otherwise. It would be as if we were being sent to school for a certain period of time and with certain schoolmates and when we had learned certain lessons we would be given a rest to evaluate our efforts and determine the next lessons. No one knows how long we will need. Some may need seventy years, others just a few months or years, to complete their work during a particular session.

Since separation from loved ones is only temporary, even this could be more easily accepted. As we begin to understand that only love is eternal and that it will always connect us with our loved ones, even after the dropping of the physical body, the pain of the separation begins to ease. With this interpretation the pain of the loss may not be avoided but chronic despair can. If we begin to understand that we are spiritual, not just physical beings, then physical separation from a loved one would be reconcilable. The great lesson of the resurrection was to provide an example of the ultimate illusion that death is.

Sickness and Pain as an Alert and Motivator

To understand how sickness and pain, both emotional and physical, can exist in a benevolent Universe another reinterpretation is necessary. Pain and sickness are not willed by God but rather miscreated by us as Divine Energy flows through us and is fractured through our filters. Physical sickness or pain is a warning system that alerts us to the fact that something is out-of-balance in our bodies, and therefore in our minds. Usually our first response to this alert is to attempt to heal the body through the use of a physical agent, i.e., drugs, surgery, therapy. These techniques can be somewhat effective, as the mind still believes in their abilities. The use of these techniques should not be abandoned if to do so would engender greater fear.

However, physical sickness is created by the mind through its emotions and thoughts. All therapy therefore is really psychotherapy (*Course*, psychotherapy, p. 1). The mind can heal the body but the body cannot heal the mind. This fact alone establishes their hierarchy. In many ways, sickness is anger, at ourselves or others, taken out on the body. The pain is an alert to remind us of this and that forgiveness and love, towards ourselves and / or others, is required for healing to occur. The alert can always be heeded in time. This is not to say that we can cure the body of the sickness, indeed we may even die from it. But we can always heal the mind of the sickness that caused the physical symptoms. A physical cure is not always possible, but inner healing is, if we choose it. We do not always know when someone's work here is completed. That is between each of us and our Creator. If we are alive our work is not yet done.

Pain is a motivator for change. When pain or the threat of pain or death is confronting us, we seem to make our greatest changes, both physically and emotionally. Pain, at least in earlier stages of a being's development, seems to be necessary to catalyze real change. At later stages of development, the joy and freedom of the release from our fears becomes the main motivator for change. If we are correctly interpreting the alert the pain is sending, we will begin to heal our minds and often cure our physical symptoms. Maybe we have experienced a loss of health or physical pain; we must then evaluate our lifestyle and change our unhealthy and self-destructive habits. A major illness might cause us to reexamine our priorities and make needed adjustments. A tremendously painful event often prompts us to become an advocate for change so that others avoid similar painful events. We may have lost a loved one or suffered a divorce, and that prompts an inner search.

The need for pain as a motivator for positive change is necessary not only for us individually, but also on a global level. Only after painfully polluting our planet have we begun environmental changes. Only after crippling our economies through fear and greed have we begun to rethink the wasteful outlay of a large percentage of the world's productivity towards war equipment we hope never to use. Only after advancing warfare to the frightening point of possible global annihilation have we begun to seriously work towards world peace.

Perceived as an alert and motivator, it is easier to understand how pain and sickness might exist in a benevolent Universe, where we all have free will to express the flow of Divine Energy through us in any manner we choose, no matter how painful or twisted. It would be an unkind and cruel God who did not offer these alerts and motivators because we could become stuck in illusions forever and never know the joy freedom from them brings. If God created a Universe without pain, sickness, and death, His Universe would be limited and we would not have free will. We could experience some things but not others.

However, not all sickness is a warning alert of an unhealed mind. Some sickness may be necessary to teach certain lessons to someone in terms of the work they are meant to do. This may be the case of young children who are in pain or ill. How have the filters of their minds become darkened at such a young age as to cause their own sickness? In these cases, it may not be the experiences of this lifetime that have affected their minds in such a way as to create an illness. For reasons that are not understandable to the outside observer, the illness or pain may be needed in the lessons they were to learn and teach. Perhaps the enhanced maturity, acceptance, and patience that is learned during an illness are major lessons for them during this lifetime. Perhaps their illness has engendered an opening of the hearts of the parents, care-givers, and other witnesses to their suffering. Though these occurrences are painful, it is only our interpretations that classify them as negative events.

Perhaps the most intense emotional pain is the loss of a loved one through death. Just reinterpreting our concept of death can make this much easier. This pain can also help to awaken us to the possibility that we are more than just our physical bodies and our connection with loved ones is more than just physical. We can come to understand that our separation from them is temporary and that our ability to connect with them may be even greater now that they are no longer bound by a physical body. Their loss can also teach us acceptance and letting go, reminding us that we are all flowing along together, in and out of bodies, but always connected by love. It may allow us the opportunity to reexamine our attachments. We may discover that some of these attachments were based on our fears of being abandoned or left without love. The pain of letting go of these attachments, especially to other people, can often be intense but the heat of their intensity can often be purifying and lead us back to our spiritual nature.

We do not always need to be alerted and motivated in a painful manner, though for a period it may be the only way to penetrate the constant distractions and illusions with which we have surrounded ourselves. As we become more aware of lessons we were sent to teach and learn, we do not need such loud alerts to remind us. As we begin to understand why we are here and glimpse the joy and lack of conflict that is available to us, such powerful motivators are no longer needed. We can even begin to ask that our lessons be delivered to us gently. We become self-motivated towards our own freedom.

Forgiveness as Healing and Release from Pain

Other forms of emotional pain are also teachers and motivators for us. Much emotional pain stems from either self-condemnation or judgment of others. We then misinterpret this pain as suitable punishment or justification for retribution for our various shortfalls or "sins." However, this pain too can be reinterpreted as a valuable teaching aid that is there to allow us to reexamine our decisions and to choose differently.

Forgiveness, both of ourselves and others, is the key to healing the mind and body and to peace of mind. Other than the obvious negative emotions (anger, jealousy, hate, resentment, guilt), and their consequential physical illnesses, there is another reason that the lack of forgiveness will always rob our peace of mind. No one who is unaware of their real nature can be at peace. If we do not forgive ourselves and others it is only because we have forgotten who we are.

If we feel ourselves to have been unfairly treated it is because we have misinterpreted both who we are and the meaning of the "offending" action. There are really only two emotions, love and fear (*Course*, text, p. 230). Even the most offensive action is just a twisted way of asking for love. This is why people who have been severely abused during childhood and experienced little love, are the greatest offenders. In their twisted way they are seeking the love they never knew. The pain they experienced is validated as justification for retribution, even if it is directed towards a stranger. Whatever the "offense" towards us, which we usually interpret as an attack, we can reinterpret this as an asking for love by a young, spiritual child, struggling to grow. The appropriate response to a fellow human who is asking for love is to give love, even when we feel attacked. This is what we are here to learn and to teach. This is what we are asked to do when we are told to love our enemies. It is the message of the crucifixion, that we can always forgive and love, even if we have been betrayed, deserted, and condemned.

The attack, the offense, is a teaching aid to show us where we are having trouble learning to love. It also exposes the fears that have caused the anger (*Course,* text, p. 202). We are never upset for the reasons that we think (*Course,* workbook, p. 8). If we interpret this asking for love as an attack by someone who has "sinned" against us, we will demand punishment or retribution. If we feel this way towards others we must feel this way towards ourselves, knowing that we too are not always loving and have "sinned" against others. As we condemn others, so we condemn ourselves. Since we do not understand that the other person is a developing spiritual being seeking love as they learn, we do not therefore understand that is also who we are. Since we feel they have sinned and deserve punishment, we feel the same about ourselves. We do not know who they are and therefore we do not know who we are. Both the anger, towards ourselves and others, and the misunderstanding of who we all really are, will continue to cause inner conflict and pain, often expressing itself through physical illness.

In time, this conflict and pain will prompt us to reexamine our interpretations and seek other interpretations that will allow us freedom from this suffering. We can each determine our own pace for this but we will all eventually seek a release from this suffering, though perhaps not during this term in school. As we begin to love and forgive ourselves, we begin to love and forgive others.

Tragic Events as Major Crossroads

Many people, when confronted with a very painful, perhaps tragic event, decide that this is proof that the Universe can be neither safe nor benevolent. This is understandable, as it is difficult to feel safe or blessed when we are in great pain. Earlier in this chapter a reinterpretation of pain and death has been offered that may allow us to view painful events in our lives from a different, more positive, perspective. Even with this reinterpretation, there are extremely painful events in our lives (a sudden death of a loved one, a divorce, a business failure, a betrayal, serious illness, etc.) that seem to test our ability to find any redeeming value from their occurrence. These events are watershed events in our lives and their power to change us is immense. These events will always cause us anguish for a period of time and pain perhaps forever. However, it is our choice whether, in the end, they have darkened our spirit or have become milestones and added greater purpose and peace to our lives.

As we begin to love and forgive ourselves, we begin to love and forgive others.

If these painful events have occurred through no "fault" of our own, i.e., a death, or illness, we tend to blame a cruel God or curse our bad luck in a random Universe. If we, or others, have had some involvement in deciding the outcome, i.e., in a divorce, a business failure, or a betrayal, we will tend to blame ourselves or the others involved. Since we have decided something "bad" has happened we feel there must be someone or something to blame. This pain then becomes validation for an attack against the perceived perpetrator, whether it is ourselves, others, God, or a random Universe. This then confirms our view that attack against ourselves or others is justified or that the Universe operates on a random or punitive basis. If we hold to this belief, we will use this event as final proof as to the punitive or random nature of the Universe. The net result of the personal "tragedy" will be more pain and confusion than growth and freedom.

The ability of these tragic events to crush the human spirit, is no greater than their ability to elevate it. These events are often the beginning of a lifelong examination of previously held beliefs. In many instances anything less than a major, usually painful, event would not have prompted such a reexamination. The result of this subsequent inner search is often greater peace of mind and sense of purpose. Though the pain of the "tragedy" may linger, we often feel it created changes in our lives for which we are grateful. The tragedy tends to refocus our priorities and remind us of what is truly important in life.

In some instances, the intense pain becomes a catalyst for a life's work or calling. Many service organizations, such as those to prevent alcohol-related accidents or locate missing children, were founded by people who had directly experienced the pain these tragedies can cause and subsequently decided to devote their lives to help prevent others from having to experience them. A story is told of a woman who watched her entire family killed in a German concentration camp, and who, after the war, dedicated her energies to the care of sick or injured children, many of whom were victims of the war. In an even greater show of courage she chose only German children to help her release all her bitterness towards the German people. In this example, the intense pain of the loss of her family was used as a teaching aid for her to learn to love, no matter how severe the apparent attack. In her learning this, she teaches it to us.

Bringing It All Together

Hopefully, these reinterpretations of life's painful events will allow us to greatly reduce the fear that is engendered when we contemplate or confront any of them. In time all fear can be removed for there is really nothing to fear. What is there to fear in a Universe where death is not final but rather a beautiful transition, and any separation from a loved one is only temporary? What is there to fear when sickness and pain and failure are valuable tools for growth and for us to uncover and understand our fears so that we may experience the joy freedom from these fears bring? What is there to fear from a totally abundant and benevolent Universe which will always provide us with all the love, safety, and material abundance that we need once we open to it? What is there to fear when we understand that we are much more than our egos and bodies—that we are Divine miracle workers on a sacred mission from our Creator? What is there to fear when all the guidance and help we need is no further than a prayer away? What is there to fear when, by choosing love instead of fear, we can know happiness and peace at each moment of our lives?

We are beginning to awaken and remember who we are. Incarnate in a physical body and assaulted by both its fears and pleasures, we had forgotten our true nature and our goal. Now we are beginning to understand we are much more than this body. Our freedom will lead us to this forgetfulness and it will lead us out again. The journey was necessary because we, as limitless beings in a limitless Universe, had to experience the physical plane, with all its pains and pleasures and its ability to create temporary amnesia. Now the veil is beginning to lift.

As the introduction to *A Course In Miracles* states: This course can therefore be summed up very simply in this way:

Nothing real can be threatened.
Nothing unreal exists.
Herein lies the peace of God.

(*Course,* text, introduction)

About the Author

Robert Roskind is a private businessman and lecturer. He owns and operates his own company and has authored five books. He has produced an acclaimed television series for PBS and his business ventures have been featured in *Newsweek, The Wall Street Journal, Money,* on *The Today Show,* and in other media. He also lectures and consults businesses and individuals on applying the principles of *A Course in Miracles* to business. He lives in Chapel Hill and Oriental, North Carolina with his wife and daughters.

If you are interested in having Robert speak to your company or organization or consult individually, he can be reached at:

Robert Roskind
Windmill Point
Oriental, North Carolina 28571